WILEY FINANCE EDITIONS

The New Science of Technical Analysis

Thomas R. DeMark

John Wiley & Sons, Inc.
New York • Chichester • Brisbane • Toronto • Singapore

This text is printed on acid-free paper.

Published by John Wiley & Sons, Inc.

This publication is designed to provide accurate and authoritative information in regard to the subject matter covered. It is sold with the understanding that the publisher and the author are not engaged in rendering legal, accounting, or other professional services. If legal advice or other expert assistance is required, the services of a competent professional person should be sought.

Library of Congress Cataloging in Publication Data:

DeMark, Thomas R., 1947–
The new science of technical analysis / Thomas R. DeMark.
p. cm. — (Wiley finance editions)
ISBN 0-471-03548-3 (acid-free paper)
1. Investment analysis. 2. Stock price forecasting. 3. Financial instruments—Prices—Forecasting. I. Title. II. Series.
HG4529.D46 1994
332.6—dc20 94-18145

Printed in the United States of America

10 9 8 7 6 5

I dedicate this book to those individuals who have contributed emotionally, physically, spiritually, inspirationally, intellectually, and professionally to my investment career. Without their influence on my life, this endeavor would never have been anything more than a mere fantasy—

To my children T.J., Carrie, Meghan, Rocke, Evan, and Dominic, for the time they sacrificed and the patience they exhibited to allow me to complete this project;

To my wife Nancy for her willingness to support my efforts and to prevent distractions;

To my father Louis and my mother Carmilla, for the direction they provided and the values they instilled;

To William R. Johnson and A. Keith Johnson, for the employment opportunity of a lifetime;

To Paul Tudor Jones and Peter Borish, for their recognition and appreciation of professional money management;

To Van Hoisington, for the fortitude and foresight to invest in the future;

To Larry Williams, for his encouragement to create and to challenge myself and for his friendship;

To Charlie ("D") DiFrancesca and John DiFrancesca, for the inspiration to excel and to accept adversity;

To David Baker, Gibbons Burke, Ed Cicosz, Leon Copperman, Joe Generalis, Thomas Henson, Anthony Kolton, Jack Kunkel, John Miller, Brian Pedersen, Dr. Guenther Pfister, John Snyder, Ron Williams, and Bernard C. Ziegler III, for their contributions to my investment career.

Preface

If you are seeking a panacea for all your trading ills, this book is not your cure. There is, in fact, no infallible investment approach. Extraneous items outside the realm of market research also contribute to a trader's performance. Specifically, considerations such as sound money management principles, including both capital preservation and strict trading discipline, are key components of trading success. The parameters of this book are limited to research, and any discussion of money management techniques and of market psychology is incidental to the presentation of market timing tools and methods. This is not to imply that a trader could not survive profitably using solely market timing models, but rather to stress the fact that other variables not addressed in this book play a vital role in distinguishing between a mediocre and an accomplished trader.

Throughout my career, I have been fortunate to have been associated as a partner, a consultant, and an employee with many of this generation's most notable investment luminaries and companies. I have advised the companies of individuals such as George Soros, Michael Steinhardt, Leon Cooperman, and Laurence Tisch; have worked as executive vice president for Paul Tudor Jones; have established a trading company with Charlie ("D") DiFrancesca; managed a futures fund with Van Hoisington, and created market timing systems with Larry Williams. In addition, I have served as a consultant to the key decision makers at various investment giants—Goldman Sachs, Citibank, Morgan Bank, Discount Corporation of New York, IBM Pension, Minnesota Mining Pension, Atlantic Richfield Pension, Trust Company of the West, New York Life, and Criterion Fund, among many others—often commanding fees in excess of $100,000 per year from each. Although these clients respected my advice, the most successful among them were, almost without exception, those who were able to blend this information with the money management skills and market experience they had acquired throughout years of professional practice. They will acknowledge that they utilize various market timing strategies but ultimately their decisions are subject to their own predilections. Unanimously, were you to ask these professionals to describe their investment style, they would say it was eclectic, relying on the information they deemed important at the time. Your question would be like an athlete's asking basketball legend Michael Jordan to describe how he was able to reverse dunk in midair. This talent is not something that is necessarily taught or learned: it's innate and nontransferable. Just as a composite of skills contributes to an athlete's ability, so does a composite of knowledge, instincts, and experience determine a money manager's capacity to perform.

Were it sufficiently simple for trading success to be translated into a series of formulas, trading would no longer be the challenge it is. It is my ambitious goal to provide you with the methodology required to systematize market timing techniques. My hope is that you will be able to integrate my research ideas and experience into your trading protocol. Many of the timing techniques that you may have previously perceived either to be deficient or to have been rendered obsolete may now become valuable to you with the enhancements I will provide.

Why have I chosen to share my research and ideas with you, given their reputed value? Let me cite an incident that occurred a few years ago. At the behest of my partner, I visited the Houston office of an individual who promoted market timing systems. Immediately upon my arrival, he engaged in a calculated campaign to sell me his services. To convince me of his alleged market timing expertise, he claimed authorship of two timing systems that I had created and my partner had offered for public sale the previous year! It was a shock to me since *I* was the one who had created these systems. Rather than argue with him regarding his representations, I departed questioning his legitimacy and his integrity. Since that incident, I have witnessed other individuals claiming ownership rights to other techniques I have created. By publishing this book, I intend to place my signature on the ideas presented, to protect my rights as creator and as owner.

I believe it is important that I make a significant contribution to the body of market timing information. Unfortunately, at the time I conducted my market research, I did not have the luxury of reviewing original work published by others; most information in the public domain was redundant and incomplete.

I offer to you a response my friend Larry Williams provided me years ago. Regardless of the importance of the market timing information you may give someone, invariably most individuals quickly become disenchanted or distracted, or they fail to possess the discipline required to effectively apply it. I would hope that you will not fall victim to these mental lapses and that your success in applying my trading techniques will prove this statement false.

I am pleased to share with you the products I have developed during my many years of market research. While I may have discussed some of these ideas at various seminars or workshops in the past, this book presents a compilation of my work for the first time. I alone am responsible for the research discussed. I think you will find this material original and timely even though some of the ideas were conceived and researched years ago. Hopefully, you will be as delighted with the book as I was in its preparation.

THOMAS R. DEMARK

Trademarks

The following are trademarks held by Thomas R. DeMark:

Countdown
D-Wave
Daily Range Projections
DeMarker
Magnet Price
Price Countdown
Price Intersector
Price Setup
Range Expansion Breakout
Range Expansion Index (REI)
REBO
Sequential
Setup
TD Breakout Qualifiers
TD Channel
TD Demand Line
TD Dollar Rated Option Ratio
TD Line Breakout
TD Line Value
TD Lines
TD New High-New Low Index
TD Points
TD Price Points
TD Price Projector
TD Rate of Change
TD Retracement Arc
TD Retracement Qualifier
TD Supply Line
TD Supply Points
Trend Factors

Foreword

When I first received a copy of Tom DeMark's new book on technical analysis, I was a bit puzzled by the title. After all, technical analysis isn't "new." I've even written a couple of books on the subject myself. After reading through the material, however, I quickly realized that the key word in the title was "science." Technical analysis has always had more art than science to it. Two chartists could look at the same chart of any given stock, and the same group of technical indicators, only to come up with two completely different conclusions. Much of technical analysis is truly "in the eye of the beholder."

For many reasons, this book is particularly timely. For one thing, technical analysis has never been more popular. The proliferation of powerful computers, supported by inexpensive software programs, put the arcane world of technical analysis at the fingertips of even the smallest investor and trader. With the growing popularity of futures and options trading—and the expansion of those trading vehicles to include stock indexes, Treasury bonds and foreign currencies—traders have been forced increasingly to fall back on technical methods to cope with such fast moving markets. Intermarket linkages between the four market sectors—commodities, bonds, currencies, and stocks—forced traders to follow a much wider universe of markets. Global linkages between financial markets also forced traders to adopt methods that required lightning-quick responses to rapid market movements—namely technical analysis.

Another major contribution to the growing popularity of technical analysis comes from the television screen. Daily business coverage on CNBC, which is seen all over the world, includes a heavy dose of technical analysis. Never before have so many people been exposed to daily explanations and analysis utilizing technical methods. The academic world has even adopted a more benign attitude, with many educational institutions encouraging students to pursue technical research.

All of which brings us back to Tom DeMark's emphasis on a more scientific approach to technical analysis. With so many people now investigating the technical approach, DeMark's call for less art and more science couldn't be more timely. Starting with a more precise way to draw trendlines, and then working his way through more creative approaches to wave analysis and moving averages to name just a few, DeMark takes a fresh look at traditional approaches and adds a few new ones of his own. In each instance, his message is to be more creative and more precise—in a word, to improve. In doing so, he raises each method to a new level.

For the past twenty years, DeMark's work as a consultant has been restricted to large institutions and many of the legendary traders in the world today. By sharing his creative ideas with us, and with his passion for precision and improvement, Tom DeMark's emphasis on the "new science" of technical analysis helps push the technical frontier another step forward. With the unprecedented attention now being paid to technical analysis, this new book couldn't have come at a better time.

JOHN J. MURPHY

John J. Murphy, author of *Technical Analysis of the Futures Markets* and *Intermarket Technical Analysis* and technical analyst for CNBC, is president of JJM Technical Advisors Inc., Oradell, New Jersey.

Acknowledgments

I would like to thank Logical Information Machines, Inc. of Chicago, Illinois (312-987-0055 or 800-546-9646) for their expert help in preparing all but one of the charts in this book. Joseph Gits spent untold hours developing the charts and William Aronin and Anthony Kolton offered help at every level.

I would also like to thank my editor at John Wiley & Sons, Myles Thompson, his assistant, Jackie Urinyi, and Karl Weber, publisher, as well as the staff at Publications Development Company of Texas.

Contents

Introduction

It's amazing how precise the formulas and the contents labels for health products must be and how closely they are monitored to ensure the physical safety of consumers. On the other hand, it is disturbing that no such prescription or safeguard exists to guarantee the financial safety of investors' assets by requiring thorough testing and analysis of the techniques employed to trade their funds. It's a sad commentary to see supposedly well-educated, trained individuals risk huge sums of money applying artistic and totally subjective methods to arrive at trading decisions. Surely enough historical and profitable observations have been made to justify the use of various market timing approaches. Unfortunately, most cases are identified retrospectively; when the human eye is trained to select only those examples that work best and to overlook the many unprofitable ones.

Too often, analysts fail to dissect techniques in order to ferret out what is important and what can contribute to their trading success. Throughout many years, I have isolated a number of the key components of various market timing approaches. With the help of charts, data, and other empirical observations, I will identify these important elements, as well as many others. This book should enable you to become a successful trader. Although it is not essential that you accept *all* the techniques and suggestions presented in order to improve your trading capability and versatility, proficiency in a few should help considerably.

There are three distinct approaches to chart analysis. The first is casual and subjective and is based on the interpretation of a price chart using "gut feel" or, more precisely, guesswork. Most traders operate on this simplest level because it requires no rigorous analysis or justification. Unfortunately, for the sake of expediency they sacrifice consistency and logic.

The second approach creates market timing indicators that identify the price levels generally associated with overbought/oversold zones. Although a number of traders subscribe at least partially to this type of analysis, typically these individuals not only limit the scope of their research to various widely followed indicators but also practice generally accepted methods of interpretation. In other words, they totally lack creativity and fail to attempt either to develop their own stable of indicators or to make improvements to existing indicators. Furthermore, they often possess inflated expectations regarding the value of these indicators and they fail to appreciate their limitations.

The most effective and most valuable approach is the development of systems that actually generate buy and sell signals. Few analysts possess the background, the experience, and the willingness to devote the time and energy necessary to acquire this expertise. I intend to discuss the evolution from the artistic first level to the sophisticated, mechanical third level, and I will highlight examples describing the benefits of applying both proven systems and disciplined techniques.

President Herbert Hoover used to remark on his relentless search for a one-armed economist who was incapable of qualifying his forecasts with a statement that began, "On the other hand, ..." The implied complaint would apply to most market analysts today. I have often observed that many analysts have a unique ability to talk out of both sides of their mouths. With the techniques I will share with you in this book, the opportunity to equivocate no longer will exist. Ideally, not only will you cease to be dependent on others' advice but also you will be equipped to assume total responsibility for all your trading activities and decisions. In other words, the proverbial "pointed finger" will be directed toward yourself. The procedures and rules that are critical to trading independence will be presented and explained in detail. For vague and poorly defined trading techniques, I will substitute definitive and clear steps to market timing success. No longer will you be afforded the luxury and the excuse of trading with a rearview mirror. The simplistic and risk-free approach of retrospectively and subjectively identifying buy and sell levels will be replaced with the skill and know-how required to evaluate entry and exit points that are prospectively and mechanically ideal. The maturation process from "chart artist" (chartist) to chart scientist will have begun in earnest.

I recommend that, as you read this book, you concentrate on and introduce into your trading regimen only those elements with which you feel comfortable and which are compatible with your trading style. Most of the techniques and ideas presented in the following chapters reinforce one another, but they are so dissimilar that you may elect to study and perfect only a few at a time. Keep in mind that these ideas evolved over a period of more than 23 years spent in market research, as both a vocation and an avocation. Consequently, mastery of these topics should not be expected immediately; they will require your undivided attention and total concentration. I suggest that you maintain a reasonable pace studying the numerous techniques and concepts presented and that you not be discouraged by an inability to totally grasp all the details and nuances of the subject matter immediately. The format in which the various topics are presented allows for both intensive and comprehensive study. At the same time, because of the diverse nature of the chapters, you are afforded the opportunity to concentrate only on areas that are of specific interest, without the necessity of referring to and understanding other unrelated information.

Most of the ideas and concepts presented throughout this book are unconventional, unorthodox, and foreign to what most traders have learned and practiced in the past. They are original, fresh, and they cover many areas of the discipline of market timing analysis. In some circles, I expect, I will be characterized as a trading iconoclast who is shattering many time-worn practices and norms. My only wish is that readers accept these novel approaches in the context in which they are both intended and presented. They are new and exciting investment timing tools designed to supplement, to upgrade, and to complement the current group of trading methods. For beginning traders, the book will provide a solid and valid foundation on which to develop a trading research background.

The techniques described in this book have been prepared and designed for a trading audience. My experience confirms that most of the concepts discussed have universal application with equal success to other fields wherein any series of data or graphic presentations are readily available and studied. I believe that almost any discipline that can be quantified and that lends itself to trend analysis is a potential candidate for this type of research discussion and application. Specifically, I have calculated retracements, projections, and objectives for data in diverse areas ranging from interest rates and other economic statistics to forecasts of the migration trends of birds. I encourage you to examine thoroughly and critically my trading techniques and, should you desire, to experiment with and explore the possibilities of their application to other fields. At the same time, I challenge you to make enhancements to my research. My biggest complaint has always been that most traders are like the split ends on football teams rather than the quarterbacks: they are capable only of receiving information, not of supplying it.

I have witnessed the evolution of market timing research from a simple Bowmar calculator to the current preoccupation with such exotic, high-technology analyses as artificial intelligence, chaos theory, optimization models, neural networks, and so on. The onslaught of this advanced mathematical theory and of elaborate computer capabilities has fostered a disinterest in uncomplicated, basic, "blue-collar" market timing techniques and devices. However, even as these sophisticated approaches have instilled a false sense of trading security, they have failed to reward their advocates with markedly improved performance results. Consequently, I predict a return to the simple, pure analytical approaches and hope that this book and the trading suggestions contained in it serve as a catalyst to expedite this revival.

Chapter

1

Trendlines

Whether a trader is a practitioner of fundamental or of technical analysis, invariably, at one time or another, he has relied on trendlines to make his forecasts. Although trendlines are universally used, it is surprising how dissimilar they are in construction and interpretation, and how subjectively they are applied. Not only is it commonplace for different analysts to draw different trendlines representing the same data during the same time period, but the same individual, on separate occasions, will also draw two totally different trendlines based on the identical information, depending on his inclination each time. Consistency and uniformity are totally lacking. Not all the trendlines can be correct—only one is. Through exhaustive, painstaking research and years of experience and application, I have arrived at an effective method to select the two critical points that are essential to the proper construction of a trendline. Once learned and applied, trendline analysis is no longer subjective; instead, it becomes totally mechanical. Trendline breakouts are precisely defined and price objectives can be easily calculated: systems can actually be created. Price gaps and large price range moves assume a significance never before imagined.

Selection of TD Points™ and Construction of TD Lines™

Supply and demand dictate price movement. Specifically, should demand exceed supply, price advances; conversely, should supply exceed demand, price declines. These are basic economic tenets accepted by all economists. In order to illustrate this phenomenon pictorially, analysts construct a descending line to represent supply and an ascending line to represent demand (see Figures 1.1 and 1.2).

The difficulty, when creating these lines, involves the specific points to select and connect (see Figure 1.3). As it often does, human nature interferes in the

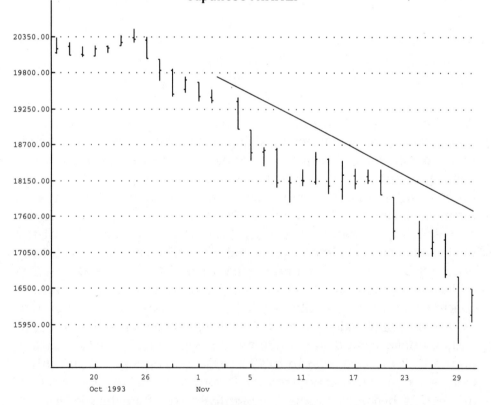

Source: Logical Information Machines, Inc. (LIM), Chicago, IL.

Figure 1.1 Note the declining price movement as defined by the downsloping "supply" line, as well as the pattern of both lower price highs and lows.

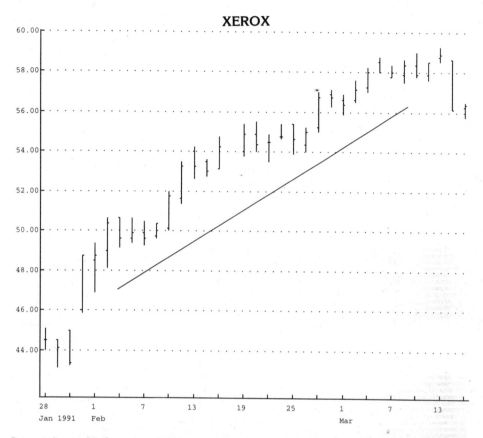

XEROX

Source: Logical Information Machines, Inc. (LIM), Chicago, IL.

Figure 1.2 Observe the ascending price movement as depicted by the up-sloping "demand" line as well as the series of both higher price highs and lows.

proper construction of these lines. For example, we are accustomed to review the historical price activity of a market—from the past to the present, with the dates reading from left to right. As a result, the demand and supply lines are drawn and extended from the left side of the chart to the right. Intuitively, this is incorrect. Recent price activity is more significant than historical movement. In other words, precision and accuracy demand that the lines be extended from right to left, with the most recent date appearing at the right side of the chart. Initially, this may appear unorthodox but, in actuality, my experience and numerous observations confirm this approach. Simplicity and ease of construction should never serve as substitutes for

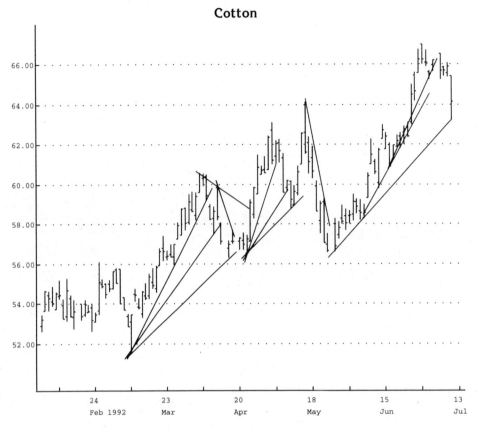

Cotton

Source: Logical Information Machines, Inc. (LIM), Chicago, IL.

Figure 1.3 It's obvious that many lines can be drawn to establish the price trend. The key elements are to select the two critical points, construct the correct trendline, and ignore the many others.

logic and accuracy. Imprecision and total disregard for detail are reflected in the common practice of constructing multiple trendlines as well as in the typically cavalier attitude of analysts who believe that one of these lines will accurately define the trend. Success in using trendlines requires both an attention to detail and a pattern of consistency.

Rather than merely presenting a set of rules designed to establish the proper method for selecting points and then connecting these points to construct a supply or a demand line, I would like to share with you a frustrating but professionally pivotal experience I had with a business colleague approximately 20 years ago. This episode proved to be a catalyst that changed my analytical life. Being fledgling traders, both he and I were consumed by the activity of the markets. Not only was the analysis of price behavior our profession, but it had also become our total obsession. Subsequent to leaving the office and returning home, we would preoccupy our evenings discussing interesting chart price patterns over the telephone. On one such occasion, we discussed at length the interplay of a series of price trends. We each drew the trendlines on our own charts. When we arrived in the office the next day and compared our respective charts, however, the lines on the charts did not even come close to resembling one another. This bothered me greatly. It was as if we had been speaking two entirely different languages to one another. I was determined to prevent this from ever happening again. It was essential that we both understood and communicated with the same vocabulary and definitions in order to avoid any further confusion and misunderstanding. Specifically, I embarked on a journey to catalog and standardize widely used market timing techniques, to improve on them, and to create my own. To this day, I strive to accomplish this goal. Trendlines were my first project.

For purposes of discussion and illustration, I will generally refer to *daily* charts and data when in fact any other time period can be easily substituted. My reasons for selecting daily information are threefold:

1. It is the most readily available and has been the most widely used time series for decades;

2. It not only relieves the trader of the necessity of constantly following the market on an intraday basis, but it also reduces considerably the risk of price revisions such as those that plague intraday data bases;

3. It increases the chance that when market signals are generated based on this information, the price fills will in actuality be executed.

Early on, I concluded that important supply price pivot points were identified once a high was recorded that was not exceeded on the upside the day immediately before as well as the day immediately after (see Figures 1.4a,b). Conversely, to define demand price pivot points, just the opposite approach was employed: a low was recorded that was not exceeded on the downside the day immediately before as well as the day immediately after (see Figure 1.5). This made sense to me; these were critical days that proved to be trend turning points in price activity. Supply overcame demand and price declined in Figures 1.4a,b, and demand overcame supply and

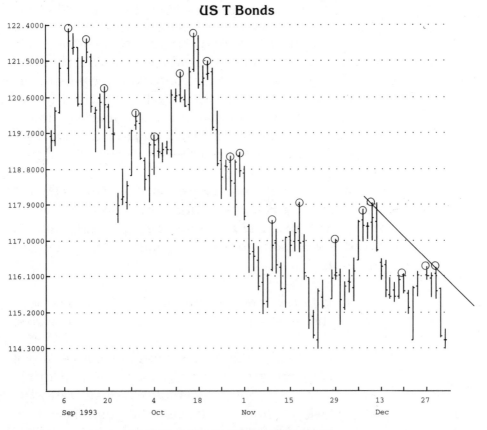

Source: Logical Information Machines, Inc. (LIM), Chicago, IL.

Figure 1.4(a) Note the highs are circled whenever that particular day's high is preceded the day before and succeeded the day after by a lower high. The supply price pivot points (TD Supply Points) are key levels since price was incapable of exceeding the resistance due to supply.

price advanced in Figure 1.5. I have labeled these key price points as TD Points. Since my research uncovered these price points, I identify them with my initials.

In Figures 1.4a,b, the two most recent peak descending TD Points™ were identified and then connected to construct the supply line (hereinafter referred to as a TD Supply Line™); in Figure 1.5, the two most recent ascending low pivot points were identified to construct the demand line (hereinafter referred to as a TD Demand Line™). It was that simple. No more excuses that I had selected the wrong points. The technique was now rigid and objective. Furthermore, the

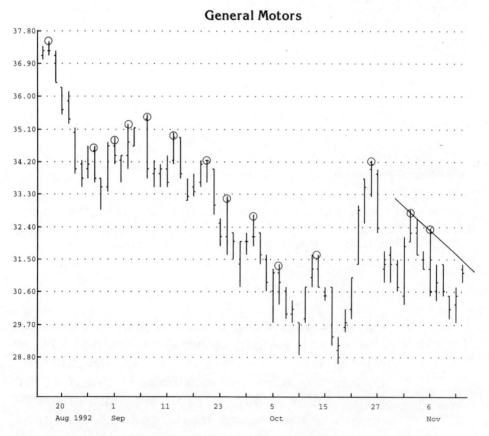

General Motors

Source: Logical Information Machines, Inc. (LIM), Chicago, IL.

Figure 1.4(b)   Supply price pivot points (TD Supply Points) are resistance points that are defined by a high that is both preceded and succeeded, on the days immediately before and after, by lower highs. These TD Price Points are identified on the chart.

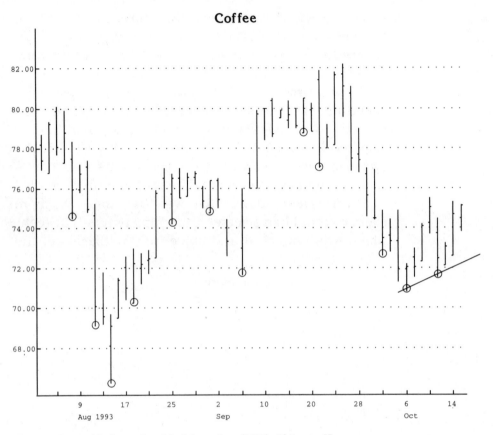

Coffee

Source: Logical Information Machines, Inc. (LIM), Chicago, IL.

Figure 1.5 Demand price pivot points (TD Demand Points) are support points that are defined by a daily price low that is both preceded and succeeded, on the day immediately before and the day immediately after, by higher lows. The TD Price Points are identified on the chart.

real attraction of this method of point selection was that it was dynamic. In other words, the market itself announced any changes in the supply–demand equilibrium equation by continuously resetting TD Points. Consequently, TD Lines are constantly being revised as more recent TD Points are being formed (see Figure 1.6). Once again, the importance of (1) the selection of the most recent TD Point and its connection to the second most recent TD Point as well as of (2) the construction of the TD Line itself becomes apparent.

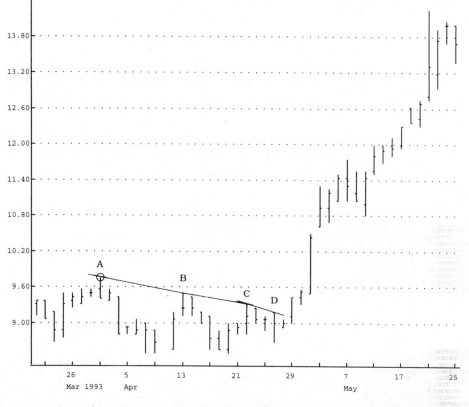

Source: Logical Information Machines, Inc. (LIM), Chicago, IL.

Figure 1.6 Four potential descending TD Supply Points are identified: A-B is the first supply line. Once TD Supply Point C is formed, however, a new supply line is constructed: B-C. Finally, when point D is defined, the supply line is revised to C-D. As you can see, the supply/demand balance is in a constant state of flux. Consequently, the supply line adapts to reflect these changes.

Refinements to TD Point Selection

I have found two modifications to the TD Point selection process to be helpful in some instances. Although they are not critical to your success in correctly selecting TD Points, they are presented for your consideration as well as for the sake of completeness.

An important factor when selecting TD Points relates to both the closes two days before the pivot high and the pivot low. In the case of the formation of a TD Point low:

1. Not only must the lows the day before and the day after be greater than the lowest low—the low in between—but the pivot low must also be less than the close two days before the low.

In other words, should a price gap separate the low one day before the lowest low and the close the day before it, that close cannot be less than or equal to the lowest low (see Figure 1.7).

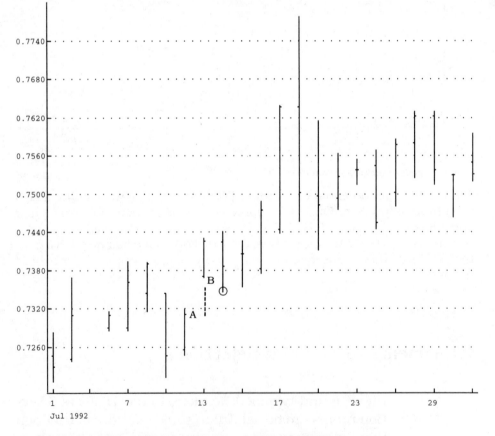

Swiss Franc

Source: Logical Information Machines, Inc. (LIM), Chicago, IL.

Figure 1.7 If the price gap defined as the distance from A to B—the price low (B) and the previous day's close (A)—is filled in, the low on the following day is no longer a demand point because the low is not less than the true low the previous day.

Conversely, in order to identify a TD Point high properly:

2. Not only must the highs the day before and the day after be less than the highest high—the high in between—but the pivot high must also be greater than the close two days before the high.

In other words, should a price gap separate the high one day before the highest high and the close the day before it, that close cannot be greater than or equal to the highest high (see Figure 1.8). As a matter of practice, some market timers differentiate between the highs and the lows that appear on a price chart and those that would appear if one were to fill in the price gaps. I coined the phrase for the former as "chart" highs and lows; and charting convention has labeled the latter as "true" highs and "true" lows.

Having worked with TD Lines for a number of years, I was able to anticipate when the TD Points selected might prove invalid. My ability to subjectively validate these points was never defined or translated into decision rules until recently. By isolating the good examples from the bad, I was able to establish prerequisites that enabled me to perfect TD Point selection. This validation process involved the relationship between the most recent pivot point low or high and the close the day immediately following it. Specifically, if the close the day after the most recent pivot point low is below the calculated value of the TD Line rate of advance, the validity of that low is suspect (see Figure 1.9). Conversely, if the close the day after the most recent pivot day high is above the calculated TD Line rate of decline for that day, the legitimacy of that high is questionable as well (see Figure 1.10).

These refinements reduce the frequency of TD Points and, consequently, of TD Lines. At the same time, however, they serve to validate both the selection of the TD Points and the utility of the TD Lines in identifying support and resistance levels as well as in facilitating the process of calculating price projections.

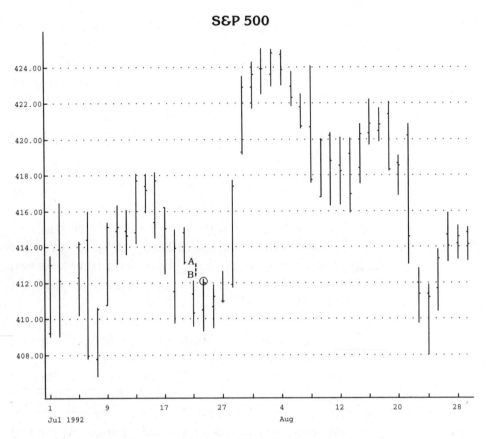

Source: Logical Information Machines, Inc. (LIM), Chicago, IL.

Figure 1.8 Were the price gap between the high and the previous day's close considered, the supply point would not exist.

Benefits Derived from Proper TD Point and TD Line Selection

I was soon to learn that many benefits to this approach had been derived as a result of both the proper identification and the application of TD Points and of TD Lines. Inexplicable price gaps that had previously appeared out of the blue took on a special meaning and significance. Often, price vaulted above a TD Supply Line precisely at its intersection with price (see Figure 1.11). Conversely, this phenomenon was observed when price gapped below a TD Demand Line (see Figure 1.12). In addition, once price exceeded a

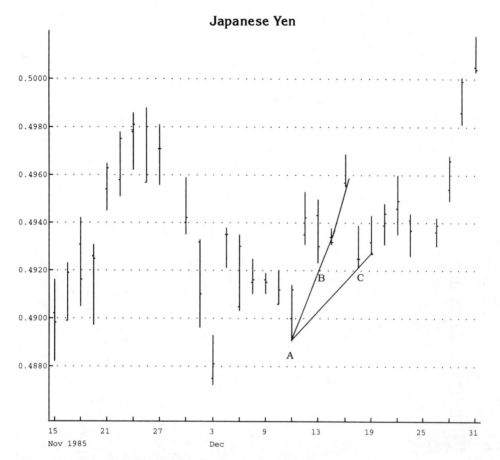

Source: Logical Information Machines, Inc. (LIM), Chicago, IL.

Figure 1.9 In this instance, the close on the day immediately after the most recent pivot point low is below the rate of ascent as defined by the demand line connecting the two most recent ascending demand points. This occurs two times on the chart: lines A-B and A-C. Although it does not invalidate the demand lines, it raises questions regarding their reliability.

TD Line, it became apparent that, in the ensuing price activity, a natural rhythm was dominant and was often predictable. For example, the extent of the price movement beneath a TD Line is often reflected in a comparable price movement above the TD Line (see Figure 1.13). Similarly, the degree of the price movement above a TD Line is often repeated beneath the TD Line (see Figure 1.14). The following discussion describes this technique in more detail.

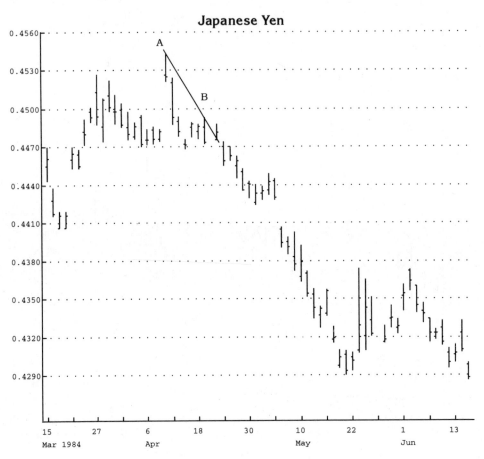

Japanese Yen

Source: Logical Information Machines, Inc. (LIM), Chicago, IL.

Figure 1.10 If the supply line constructed by connecting supply points A and B is extended, it intersects the day after supply point B, below that day's close. As you can see, a holiday gap appears on the chart and shifts price activity somewhat, but even if the chart is adjusted to accommodate this fact, the close one day after point B exceeds the line. Consequently, the value of that particular line is questionable.

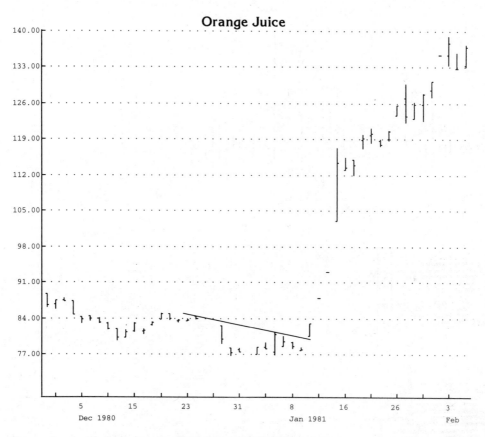

Source: Logical Information Machines, Inc. (LIM), Chicago, IL.

Figure 1.11   See how price gapped upside above the TD Supply Line on the opening, and remained above all day.

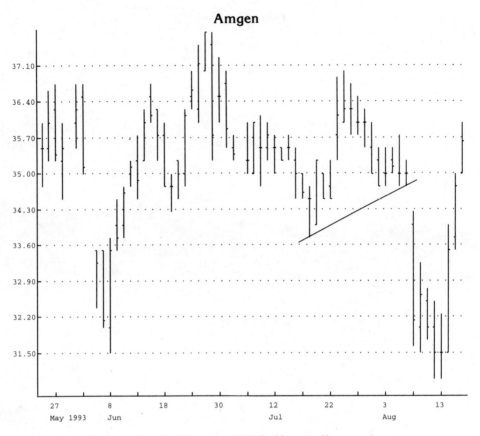

Source: Logical Information Machines, Inc. (LIM), Chicago, IL.

Figure 1.12 Observe how price opened below the TD Demand Line.

Source: Logical Information Machines, Inc. (LIM), Chicago, IL.

Figure 1.13   The price movement beneath the TD Supply Line A-B repeated only in reverse, once price exceeded the TD Line upside. The difference in price between the lowest price beneath the TD Line and the TD Line value on the same day is added to the breakout to arrive at a price objective. Specifically, price X on the TD Supply Line A-B is precisely above point Y, which is the lowest price recorded beneath the A-B Supply Line. By adding that value to the breakout above the A-B Supply Line, price projection Z is calculated.

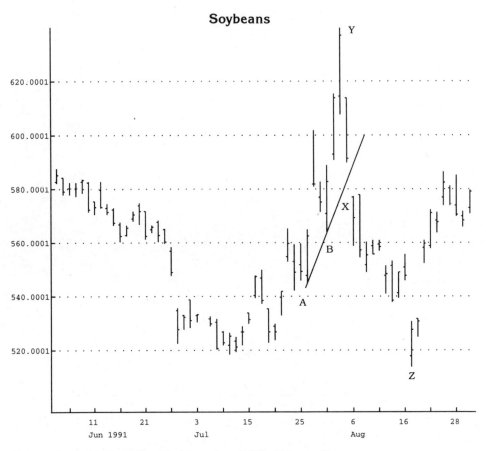

Source: Logical Information Machines, Inc. (LIM), Chicago, IL.

Figure 1.14   Price movement above TD Demand Line A-D is repeated in reverse on the downside, once the TD Line is penetrated. By calculating the difference between point Y—the highest price above the TD Line—and Point X—the specific price on the TD Line immediately beneath it—and by subtracting that value from the breakout below the A-B Demand Line, price projection Z is determined.

Price Projections

At the time I began to experiment with drawing trendlines on charts, I observed that if the price activity presented on the entire chart were bisected with a line separating, by an equal amount, extreme prices above and below that line, prices would often be drawn to and be repelled by that line (see Figure 1.15). I was fascinated. With a limited knowledge of trendlines, I

S&P 100 OEX

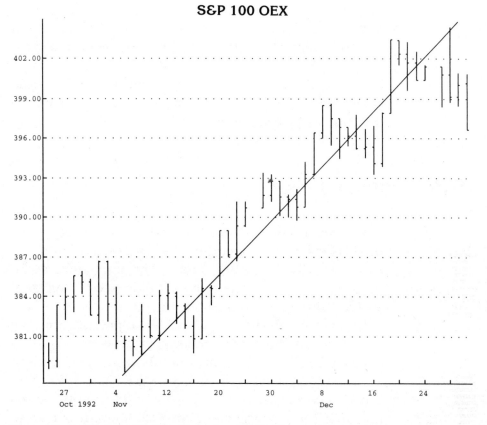

Source: Logical Information Machines, Inc. (LIM), Chicago, IL.

Figure 1.15   The price activity is attracted to the line that bisects the price movement.

continued to pursue the magnetic properties of this line. Having reviewed a considerable number of charts, I isolated as many common denominators as I could identify. You might say that this effort was both a precursor and a "back door" introduction to TD Lines. I mention this only to illustrate how I uncovered the unique property of symmetry in price movement.

Earlier, I discussed the selection of TD Points and the construction of TD Lines. Once you are comfortable with the procedures required to perform these exercises, the phenomenon of price symmetry becomes apparent. Careful inspection reveals that the differences between extreme price points immediately above a TD Demand Line and the TD Demand Line itself, as well as immediately below a TD Supply Line and the TD Supply Line itself, replicate themselves once the TD Line is penetrated (see the discussion of TD Breakout Qualifiers in the last section of this chapter). Although the pattern itself is never precisely repeated, the extent of the movement both above and below the TD Line often is, and this behavior is what I describe as price symmetry.

TD Price Projectors

There are three distinct methods to calculate price projections once a trendline is penetrated validly; I call them TD Price Projectors. The particular technique selected is a function of the degree of precision and accuracy required by the user.

TD Price Projector 1, the least precise and the easiest to calculate, is as follows: when price advances above a declining TD Line, usually price continues to advance to at least a price level equivalent to the distance between the lowest price value beneath the TD Line and the TD Line value directly above it, added to the TD Line value on the day of the breakout to the upside. What may sound complex when described in words is very simple when viewed on the chart (see Figure 1.16).

Conversely, the identical symmetry is apparent when price declines below an ascending TD Line. Usually, price continues to decline to at least a price level equivalent to the distance from the highest price value above the TD Line to the TD Line value directly beneath it, subtracted from the TD value on the day of the breakout to the downside (see Figure 1.17). Often, visual inspection will allow the user to forecast approximate price objectives; most traders require more precision, however. Basic arithmetic will enable the user to calculate the rate of change of a TD Line simply by dividing the difference between the two TD Points by the number of days between them (excluding non-trading days). Further, by multiplying the additional number of trading days from the most recent TD Point

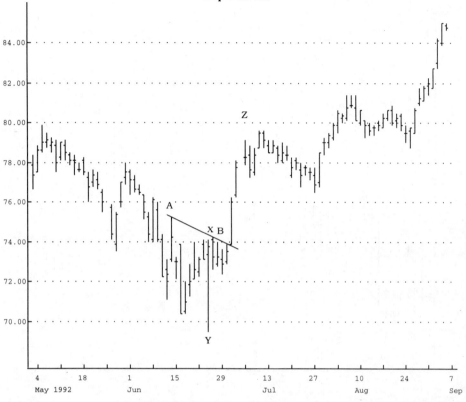

Source: Logical Information Machines, Inc. (LIM), Chicago, IL.

Figure 1.16 See how price gapped above A-B TD Supply Line and how by adding the difference between X—the value of the TD Line immediately above Y—and Y—the lowest price beneath the A-B Line—the price projection Z is determined.

to that precise point at which the TD Line is penetrated by the rate of change, the exact breakout value can be calculated (see Table 1.1). To that breakout value, the difference between the TD Line and the trough/peak immediately below/above—depending on whether it is a buy or a sell-can be added or subtracted to arrive at a price objective. Once again, what may appear complicated becomes much clearer when displayed on the charts (see Figures 1.18 and 1.19).

TD Price Projector 2 is somewhat more complex. For example, in the case in which price exceeds a declining TD Line, instead of selecting the lowest price

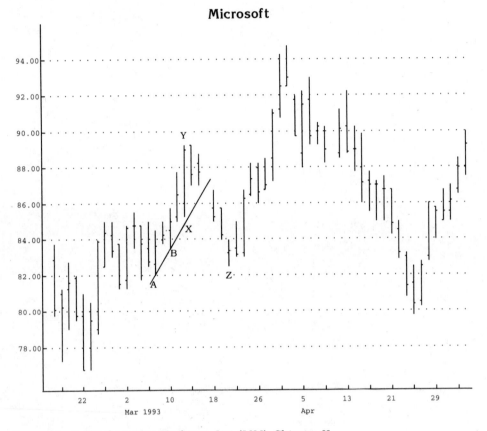

Source: Logical Information Machines, Inc. (LIM), Chicago, IL.

Figure 1.17   In an uptrending market, TD Price Projector 1 concentrates on the extreme price high above the TD Demand Line. In this instance, price opened beneath A-B TD Demand Line and proceeded to satisfy price objective Z, which is calculated by subtracting the difference between the highest price above A-B Demand Line (Y) and the A-B value (X) on that same day from the price breakout.

beneath the TD Line and adding that value to the breakout point, there is a slight variation. The intra-day low price on the day of the lowest closing price beneath the TD Line is selected. Often, the lowest intraday low is recorded on the same day as the lowest close, so there exists no difference between TD Price Projectors 1 and 2; but, in those instances when the lowest close day and the lowest low day are not coincident, the adjustment is made.

Some examples will illustrate the distinctions between the two methods (see Figures 1.20 through

Table 1.1   Rate of Change Calculation of TD Line

1. Count the number of days from the most recent TD Point to the second most recent TD Point.

2. Calculate the price difference between the two TD Points.

3. Divide the difference between the two TD Points by the number of trading days separating the two TD Points to arrive at the daily rate of advance (rate of decline).

4. Multiply the rate of advance (rate of decline) by the number of trading days to the breakout price in order to calculate the exact breakout price for purposes of arriving at a precise price objective.

5. Identify both the highest high above an ascending TD Line (the lowest low below a descending TD Line) and the value of the TD Line immediately below the highest high (above the lowest low). Next, calculate the difference between the highest high (lowest low) and the TD Line, and subtract that value from (add to) the breakout price.

1.22). As you can readily see, using the intraday low as the reference point, regardless of the close that day relative to all other closes beneath the TD line, as TD Price Projector 1 requires, is considerably more liberal and simpler to calculate. On the other hand, TD Price Projector 2, using the intraday low of the lowest close day, is a little more difficult in arriving at a price objective once a declining TD Line is exceeded upside. Conversely, to arrive at downside price projections when an ascending TD Line is broken, the reverse procedure is employed (see Figures 1.23 and 1.24). In this case, the key day to concentrate on is the highest close day or, more precisely, the intraday high that particular day. Although it may appear that TD Price Projector 2 is more precise and conservative than Projector 1, this is not always the case. For example, if the rate of advance or decline is particularly steep and the lowest close in the case of a downtrend or the highest close in the case of an uptrend—the reference day for Projector 2—occurs before the intraday low or intraday high, then the price objective for Projector 2 is greater. Conversely, if the low or the high close day beneath or above the trendline occurs subsequent to recording the intraday low or high, then Projector 2 is

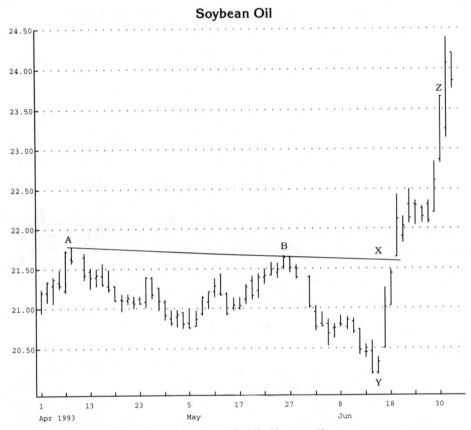

Soybean Oil

Source: Logical Information Machines, Inc. (LIM), Chicago, IL.

Figure 1.18 In a declining market, TD Price Projector 1 concentrates on the extreme low price beneath the TD Supply Line. In order to arrive at a price objective Z, calculate the difference between X—the value on the A-B TD Supply Line—and Y—the lowest price recorded beneath A-B Supply Line prior to the price breakout—and add that value to the price breakout to arrive at the price objective. In strong markets, secondary price projections can also be made by multiplying the difference by 2.

Caterpillar

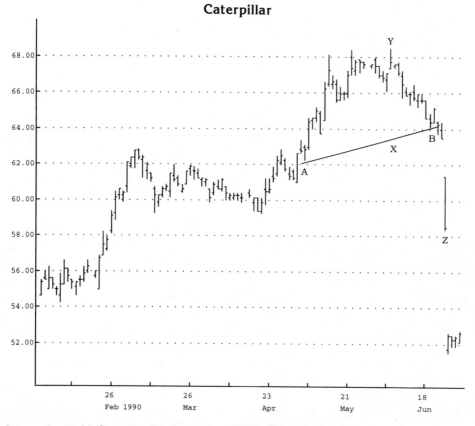

Source: Logical Information Machines, Inc. (LIM), Chicago, IL.

Figure 1.19   Once the A-B TD Demand Line is constructed, TD Price Projector 1 requires that the price objective be calculated by subtracting value X—the price on the TD Demand Line on the day the peak price (Y) above the Demand Line is recorded—from Y and then subtracting the resulting value from the breakout to arrive at Z price objective.

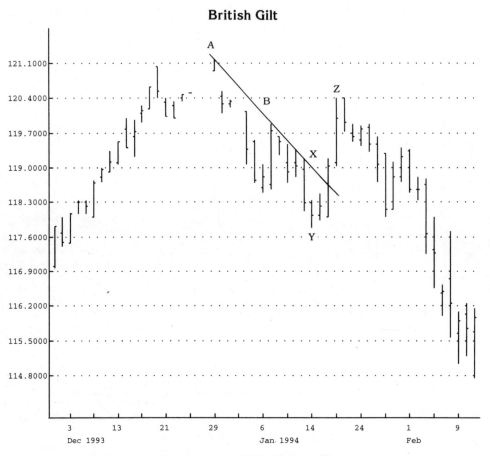

British Gilt

Source: Logical Information Machines, Inc. (LIM), Chicago, IL.

Figure 1.20 Note, in this example, TD Price Projector 2 is the same as TD Price Projector 1 because the lowest close day (Y) recorded below TD Supply Line A-B is on the same day as the lowest low (Y).

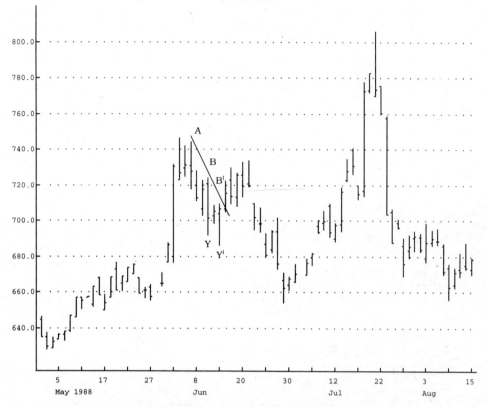

Source: Logical Information Machines, Inc. (LIM), Chicago, IL.

Figure 1.21 TD Price Projector 2 is not the same as TD Price Projector 1 in this example because the lowest close (Y) below TD Supply Line A-B is not on the same day as the lowest low (Y'). Even though the breakout point is the same value, the difference between Y and the value immediately above it on Supply Line A-B is different from the difference between Y' and the value immediately above it on Supply Line A-B. Consequently, the price objectives are not the same.

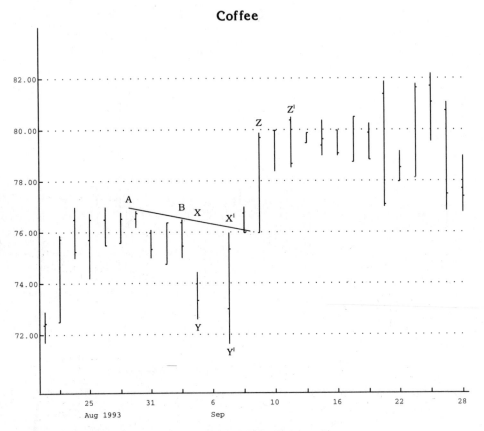

Source: Logical Information Machines, Inc. (LIM), Chicago, IL.

Figure 1.22 The price objectives (Z and Z'), arrived at by subtracting the lowest low (Y') beneath Supply Line A-B and the low on the lowest close (Y) beneath Supply Line A-B from the X and X' values on the A-B line, are not the same in this case because the lowest close and the lowest low do not occur on the same day. Thus the distinction between TD Price Projectors 1 and 2.

Coffee KC

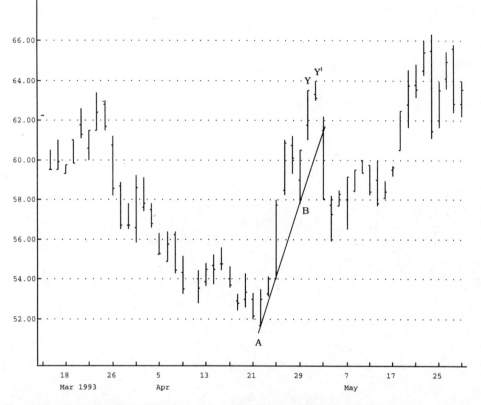

Source: Logical Information Machines, Inc. (LIM), Chicago, IL.

Figure 1.23   TD Demand Line A-B defines two different downside price objectives (Z' and Z) because the highest high day above the Demand Line (Y') is not the same day as the highest close day (Y). This differentiates TD Price Projectors 1 and 2.

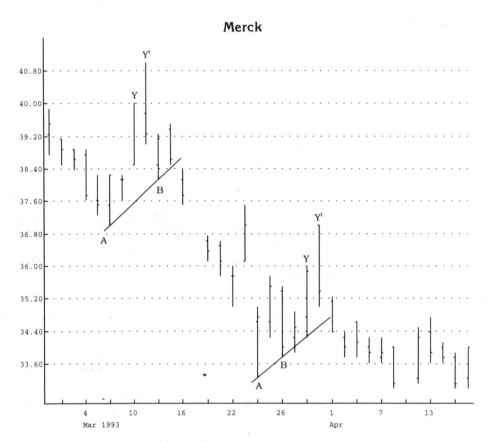

Source: Logical Information Machines, Inc. (LIM), Chicago, IL.

Figure 1.24   In both instances on the chart, lines A-B define the TD Demand Line, but the highest close above the TD Line (Y) and the highest intraday high above the TD Line (Y') do not occur on the same day. Consequently, the price objectives for TD Price Projectors 1 and 2 are not the same.

less. Personally, I prefer Projector 1 to Projector 2, but I believe that Projector 2 is valid and is a viable option.

TD Price Projector 3 is more conservative generally than the prior two methods. To calculate the price projection value in the instance of a declining TD Line, merely calculate the difference between the TD Line and the CLOSE of the lowest intraday low day immediately beneath it, NOT the intraday low itself (see Figures 1.25 through 1.27). The major distinction I wish to make relates to the intraday low and the close on the day of the intraday low. By definition, this approach is likely the most accurate

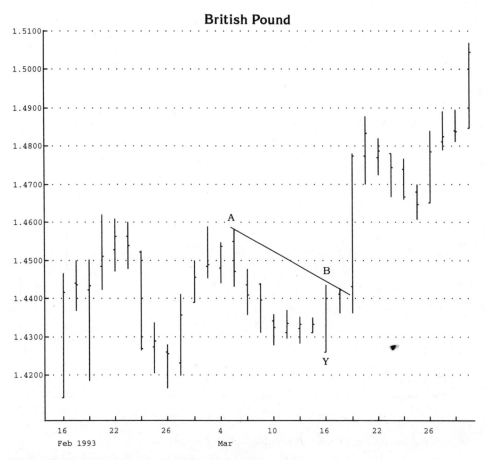

British Pound

Source: Logical Information Machines, Inc. (LIM), Chicago, IL.

Figure 1.25 TD Price Projector 3 is conservative, and its price objective is generally realized prior to fulfillment of the price objectives for TD Price Projectors 1 and 2. This example demonstrates the selection of points for TD Price Projector 3. Note the close on the lowest day (Y) is near to the Supply Line A-B and, consequently, a lower target is generated once price breaks out above the TD Supply Line.

in projecting prices because it usually yields the smallest returns. In order to reach the price targets established by TD Price Projector 1, the price objective generated by TD Price Projector 3 must have also been hit. Generally, this same observation applies to TD Price Projector 2, that is, the TD Price Projector 3 price target is realized first. Conversely, to project downside targets given a penetration of an ascending TD Line, the opposite procedure is conducted. The difference between the closing price of the highest

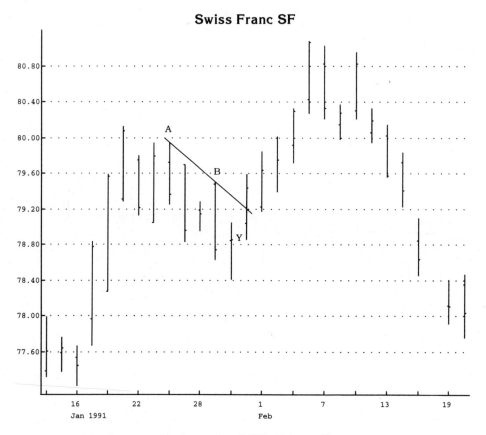

Source: Logical Information Machines, Inc. (LIM), Chicago, IL.

Figure 1.26 Once again, the upside price objective is muted because of the high close on the lowest low day relative to the Supply Line.

intraday high day above the TD Line and the TD Line value immediately beneath it is calculated (see Figures 1.28 and 1.29). Once again, I emphasize the intraday high and the close on the day of the intraday high.

Of the three approaches presented to make price projections, TD Price Projector 3 is the most precise and the most conservative. Through experimentation, you should be able to select the approach with which you are most comfortable. I highly recommend that, regardless of which one you might select, you shave one price tick from the high, low, and TD Line when calculating the price projection, to compensate for rounding off and to ensure the likelihood of the price

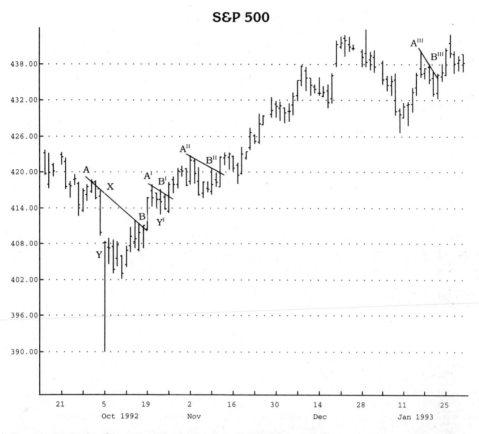

Source: Logical Information Machines, Inc. (LIM), Chicago, IL.

Figure 1.27 This chart highlights numerous instances in which TD Price Projector 3 yields lower price targets than TD Price Projectors 1 and 2 because the close of the intraday low beneath the TD Supply Line (A-B) is used.

target's being realized. Specifically, when breaking an upsloping TD Line, subtract one tick from the high or the close, depending on the method used, and add one tick to the TD Line. Conversely, when breaking a downsloping TD Line, subtract one tick from the TD Line, and add one tick to the low or the close, depending on the method used.

To fully comprehend the differences among the three TD Price Projectors, you should study Table 1.2, which summarizes the various similarities and differences.

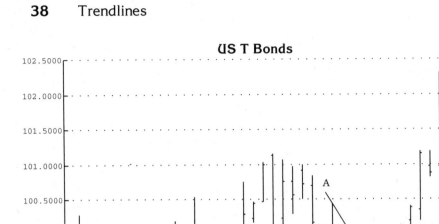

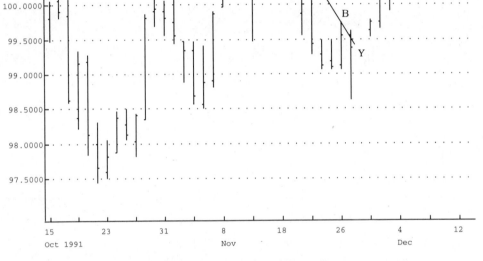

Source: Logical Information Machines, Inc. (LIM), Chicago, IL.

Figure 1.28 Unfortunately, by using TD Price Projector 3, conservative price projections are made. As in this example, should the close on the lowest intraday low day beneath the TD Supply Line be positioned in the area of the high for the day, the price objective is less than if the close were positioned closer to the low for that day.

What Could Go Wrong?

No technique is perfect. Forecasting price movements, after all, cannot be that easy. What unexpected situations could arise? Three potential developments might occur, all of which can be dealt with simply:

1. A contradictory signal could be generated by a penetration of an opposing TD Line. This would effectively nullify the active TD Line

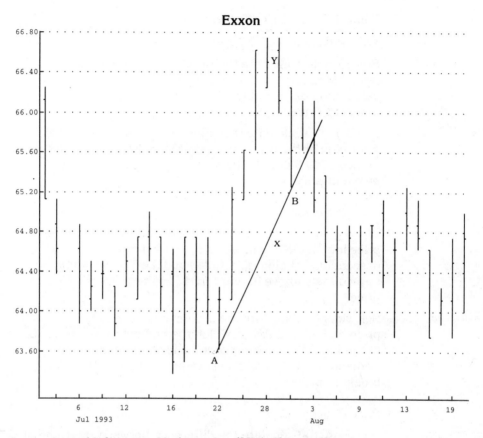

Source: Logical Information Machines, Inc. (LIM), Chicago, IL.

Figure 1.29 TD Price Projector 3 requires that the difference between the close of the highest intraday high day above the A-B Line (Y) and the value of the A-B point (X) on that same day be subtracted from the downside breakout to arrive at the price objective.

breakout and instate in its place, as the prevailing trend, the new TD Line breakout in the opposite direction. This is the most common way for a price trend to be terminated and for a price objective to be negated (see Figure 1.30).

2. The initial indication of a valid TD Line breakout may be just plain false or may be reversed by an unexpected news event that dramatically shifts the supply–demand balance. This becomes immediately apparent when the open

Table 1.2 TD Price Projectors

Price Projector 1:

Buy Signal—Calculate the difference between the lowest price low below the descending TD Line and the TD Line value immediately above it, and add that value to the breakout price.

Sell Signal—Calculate the difference between the highest price high above the ascending TD Line and the TD Line value immediately below it, and subtract that value from the breakout price.

Price Projector 2:

Buy Signal—Calculate the difference between the intraday price low on the day in which the lowest close below the descending TD Line is recorded and the TD Line value immediately above it, and add that value to the breakout price.

Sell Signal—Calculate the difference between the intraday price high on the day in which the highest close above the ascending TD Line is recorded and the TD Line value immediately below it, and subtract that value from the breakout price.

Price Projector 3:

Buy Signal—Calculate the difference between the close of the lowest intraday low below the descending TD Line and the TD Line value immediately above it, and add that value to the breakout price.

Sell Signal—Calculate the difference between the close of the highest intraday high above the ascending TD Line ahd the TD Line value immediately below it, and subtract that value from the breakout price.

for the next day is recorded: and, on the opening, it either exceeds downside the value of the active descending TD Line, which was previously penetrated, and price continues to decline; or it gaps downside on the opening and, on the close, breaks below the descending TD Line. Conversely, the breakout is suspect when, on the next day, either the open or the close is recorded and either exceeds upside with a gap the value of the ascending TD Line

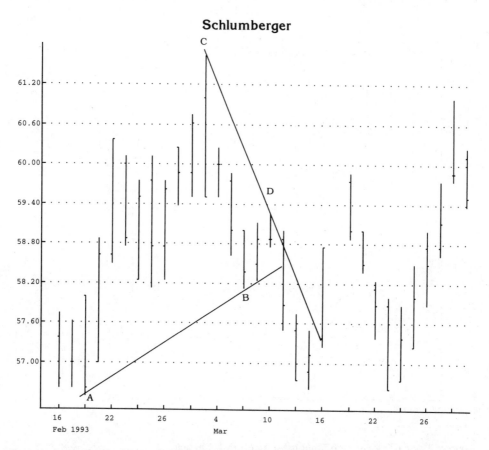

Schlumberger

Source: Logical Information Machines, Inc. (LIM), Chicago, IL.

Figure 1.30 Note that the objective of Price Projector 1 had not been fulfilled for the breakout below TD Line A-B by the time an upside breakout of TD Supply Line C-D took place. Consequently, the downside price objective based on the penetration of the Demand Line A-B is no longer active.

it previously penetrated, and price continues to advance (see Figures 1.31 and 1.32). To reduce the financial risk associated with just such unforeseen events, a stop loss can be installed once price opens on the ensuing day.

3. The fulfillment of a price objective defined by the breakout above or below a TD Line could disqualify an active trend. Such occurrences were discussed thoroughly earlier.

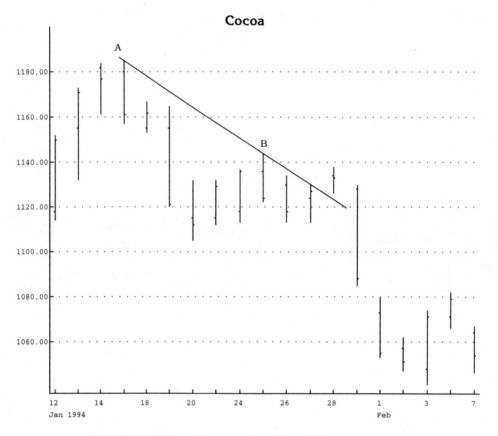

Source: Logical Information Machines, Inc. (LIM), Chicago, IL.

Figure 1.31 Although the TD Supply Line A-B was exceeded, on the day following the breakout the opening price was below the breakout day's close and it proceeded to immediately decline below the extended A-B Line. This price activity invalidates the breakout.

TD Lines of a Higher Magnitude

The TD Lines described and discussed above are of a level 1 magnitude, that is, each TD Point used to construct them required no more than three days to be defined—a high immediately preceded and succeeded by a lower high (or a low immediately preceded and succeeded by a higher low). The TD Line created by connecting two TD Points is of short duration, due to the fact that construction of as few as five highs (in

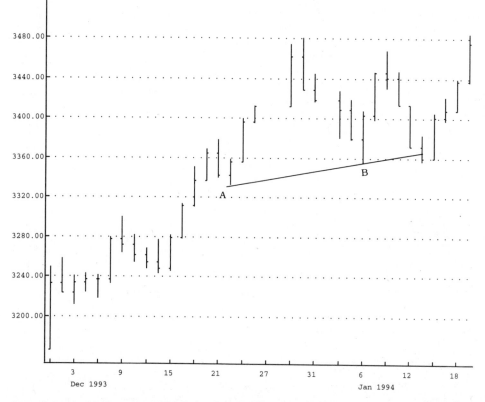

Fin. Times Index (FTSE)

Source: Logical Information Machines, Inc. (LIM), Chicago, IL.

Figure 1.32   See how price failed to decline on the day following the penetration of the TD Demand Line A-B. In fact, price opened the following day unchanged and continued to advance from that price level above the extended A-B Line, thus nullifying the breakout.

the case of a TD Supply Line) or five lows (in the case of a TD Demand Line) could require two pivot points and immediately surrounding days. A trader may wish a longer-term perspective. To satisfy this requirement, I experimented with higher-level TD Points and Lines, and realized worthwhile results.

To draw a TD Line of level 2 magnitude, a minimum of five days is required to identify each TD Point—a high immediately surrounded on both sides by two lower highs (or a low immediately surrounded

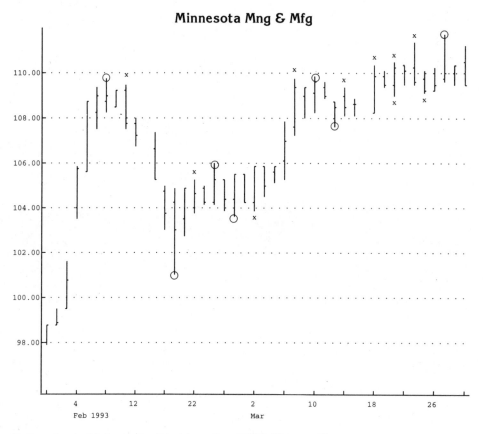

Minnesota Mng & Mfg

Source: Logical Information Machines, Inc. (LIM), Chicago, IL.

Figure 1.33 As you can see, level 3 magnitude TD Points are identified with a circle surrounding the high (low). [By definition, these are also level 1 magnitude TD Points as well. Those highs and lows marked with an "X" are level 1 points but do not qualify as level 3 because the highs (lows) all three days immediately before and immediately after are not lower highs (higher lows).]

on both sides by two higher lows). Similarly, a TD Line of level 3 magnitude would require a total of at least seven days for each, and so on for TD Lines of higher levels. It is correct to say that all TD Points of a magnitude greater than level 1 are also level 1 TD Points; but all do not qualify as active level 1 TD Line Points because, as discussed earlier, only the two most recent points are considered valid. To visualize this distinction, refer to Figures 1.33 and 1.34.

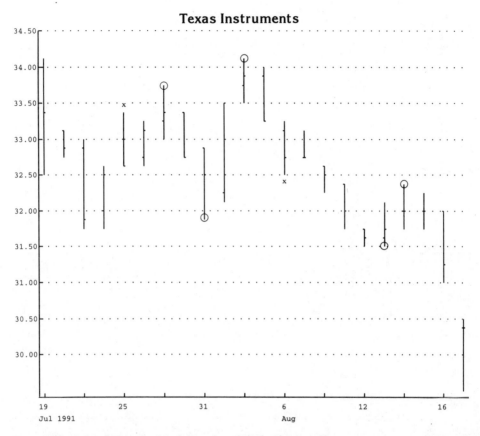

Source: Logical Information Machines, Inc. (LIM), Chicago, IL.

Figure 1.34   The distinction between level 1 magnitude TD Points ("X") and level 2 magnitude TD Points (circles) are apparent on this chart. Whereas level 1 requires merely a lower high (higher low) the days immediately before and after, level 2 requires two lower highs (higher lows) the two days immediately before and after.

Regardless which TD Line level of magnitude is selected, the same requirements exist as are described above for both TD level 1 Points and Lines. The only exception is the number of days required to define the TD Points. Similarly, the identical TD Price Projectors are used. It has generally been my preference, however, to follow level 1 magnitude TD Lines.

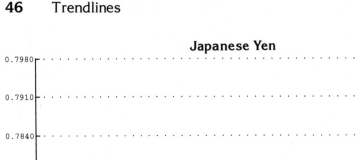

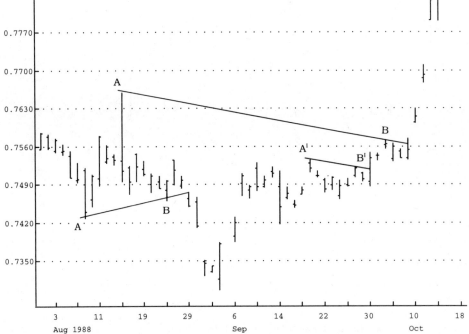

Source: Logical Information Machines, Inc. (LIM), Chicago, IL.

Figure 1.35 By awaiting the formation of a TD Point of a higher level of magnitude, lower-level TD Lines that are valid are forfeited. This chart illustrates two examples of valid breakouts that would have been identified had the points selected been level 1 or level 2 and not level 3 (see line A-B), and one example that would have been valid had level 1 been selected and not level 2 (see A'-B').

I have two primary reasons for concentrating on the basic TD Line:

    1. As the level of magnitude increases, often the breakout occurs before the most recent TD Point is completely formed, and the trading opportunity is forfeited; consequently, the exercise becomes a game of "beat the clock" (see Figure 1.35).

Gold

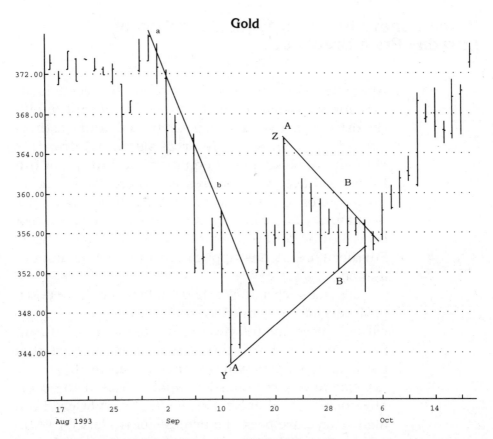

Source: Logical Information Machines, Inc. (LIM), Chicago, IL.

Figure 1.36 TD Demand Line A-B (level 2) is active until price exceeds TD Supply Line A-B (level 2) upside. (Note how the breakout above the first TD Supply Line a-b correctly predicted the subsequent price movement and price objective.)

2. As the level of magnitude increases, the likelihood of realizing the price objective before a contradictory signal occurs is reduced proportionately.

Occasionally, I will examine a higher-level TD Line to determine the trend defined by the TD Line and thereby to confirm that the TD Line I am using is consistent; in other words, I will refer to it to confirm my market outlook (see Figure 1.36).

Revolutionary Breakthrough: Validation of Intraday Price Breakouts

After the TD Points have been properly selected, the TD Line has been correctly drawn from right to left, the price objective has been calculated, and the three possible outcomes—(1) reversal signal, (2) dramatic shift in supply–demand equation, and (3) price fulfillment—have been addressed, there is one additional factor to consider: validation of intraday price breakouts. This element is significant. It is a major contribution to the study of market timing analysis. Furthermore, it has application to other techniques as well.

It's not surprising to hear that traders have taken positions on presumed trendline breakouts only to witness price fail and reverse and to incur significant losses. What is hard to understand, however, is that these same traders will continue to repeat this futile exercise and never question what causes it to occur. The incidence of false breakouts has always been high. They have been the nemesis of traders for years and have often been the excuse for totally abandoning the use of trendlines. The creation of TD Lines alleviates this problem somewhat, but invalid breakouts do occur occasionally. Heretofore, no method has been devised to differentiate between valid and invalid price breakouts.

Many years ago, I was involved in similar situations, became frustrated, and was determined to develop rules that would qualify TD Line breakouts. I was convinced that the TD Lines drawn were valid. I searched for a common denominator associated with both the good and the bad signals. It was not an easy task. The conclusions I made were startling and, at the same time, logical and simple. These were my findings.

I discovered three TD Breakout Qualifiers—two patterns occurring the day before a suspected breakout and the other pattern occurring the day of the breakout. Specifically, I concluded that if a particular

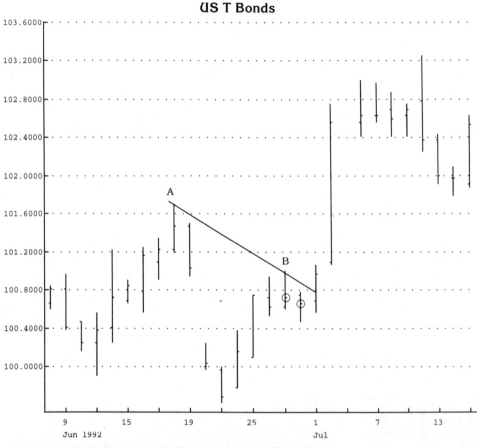

Source: Logical Information Machines, Inc. (LIM), Chicago, IL.

Figure 1.37 Note that the closing price on the day immediately before the breakout to the upside was a down close versus the previous day's close. This pattern suggests an oversold condition prior to the breakout, which is a positive formation.

market or index is oversold/overbought the day before a breakout, the chances are increased that the buying pressure/selling pressure would not be dissipated subsequent to the breakout, thus merely creating the illusion of continued strength/weakness.

I experimented with numerous conditions precedent to a breakout and found that if the close the day before an upside breakout is down, the likelihood is increased that the intraday breakout will be valid and intraday entry is warranted—TD Breakout Qualifier 1 (see Figure 1.37). Further, if the close of

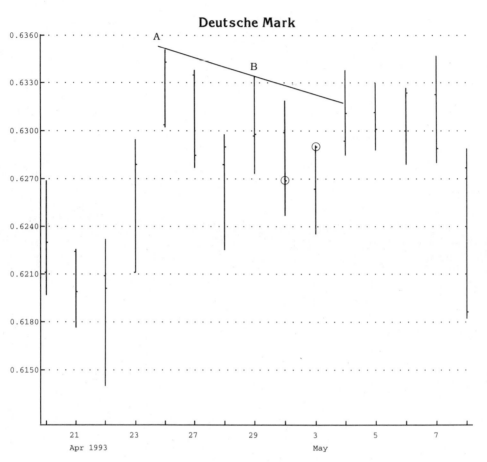

Deutsche Mark

Source: Logical Information Machines, Inc. (LIM), Chicago, IL.

Figure 1.38 Observe that the close on the day prior to the upside breakout was an up close, thus indicating an overbought condition and the likelihood of a breakout failure.

the day prior to the upside breakout is up, the possibility of a false move exists (see Figure 1.38). Conversely, if the day before a downside breakout is up, the likelihood is increased that the intraday breakout is valid and intraday entry is warranted (see Figure 1.39). Further, if the close the day prior to the downside breakout is down, the likelihood of a false move exists (see Figure 1.40).

An exception to the requirement that the close prior to an upside breakout be down and the close prior

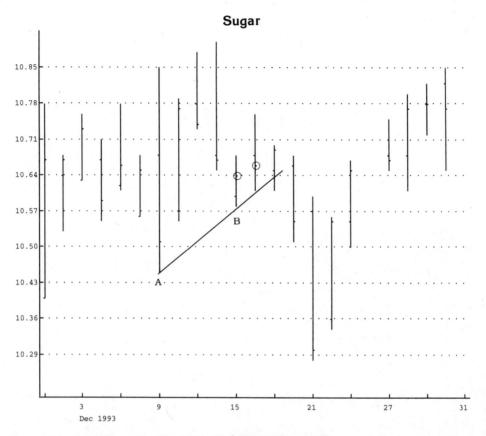

Source: Logical Information Machines, Inc. (LIM), Chicago, IL.

Figure 1.39 Note that the close on the day prior to the downside breakout was up, thus indicating a short-term overbought state and the likelihood of a valid breakout downside.

to a downside breakout be up was uncovered when an analysis of successful breakouts showed that not only would an oversold/overbought close qualify entry, but so would an open above a declining TD Line or an open below an ascending TD Line—TD Breakout Qualifier 2 (see Figures 1.41 and 1.42). This occurrence would suggest excessive strength/weakness and would justify entry at that opening price regardless of the previous day's close disqualifying the entry.

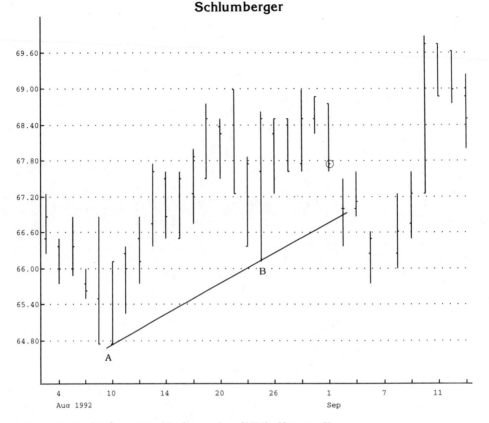

Source: Logical Information Machines, Inc. (LIM), Chicago, IL.

Figure 1.40   Notice that the close prior to the downside penetration of the A-B TD Demand Line was down, thus suggesting a false breakdown.

TD Qualifier 3 is similar to TD Qualifier 1 to the extent that it is based on price activity during the day prior to a breakout. In this case, however, the difference between the high and the close on the day prior to a trendline downside penetration is subtracted from that day's close to arrive at a supply value. The difference between the close and the low on the day prior to a trendline upside penetration is added to that day's close to arrive at a demand value (see Figures 1.43 and 1.44). If the ascending trendline is below the supply value and price exceeds the trendline, the price decline should accelerate and intraday action is warranted. Conversely, if the descending trendline is above the demand value and price exceeds the trendline, the price advance should accelerate and intraday

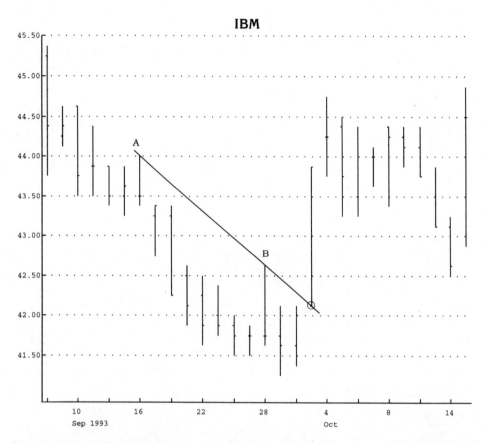

Source: Logical Information Machines, Inc. (LIM), Chicago, IL.

Figure 1.41 Observe that the opening price exceeded the TD Supply Line, thus validating a breakout.

action is warranted. Examples of TD Breakout Qualifier 3 are presented in Figures 1.45 and 1.46. Table 1.3 further describes the Qualifiers.

As presented in this chapter, TD Points are objectively defined and, when properly connected, they create TD Lines. When TD Breakout Qualifiers are introduced and the TD Lines are penetrated, legitimate price breakouts are identified and price targets can be derived. It has never been so simple. Guesswork and lack of consistency are eliminated totally. Uniformity in construction, in application, and in interpretation has been accomplished. The successful identification of trends and of trend reversal points is complete.

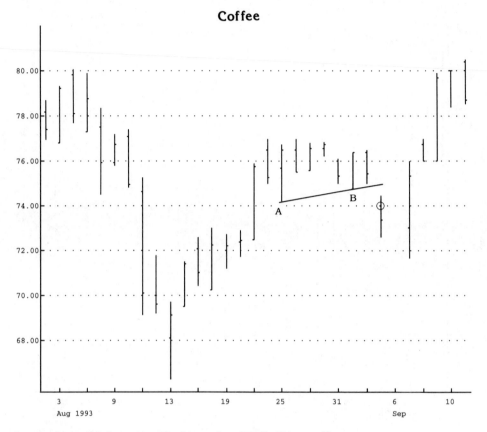

Source: Logical Information Machines, Inc. (LIM), Chicago, IL.

Figure 1.42 See how price gapped on the open below the TD Demand Line, confirming a breakout.

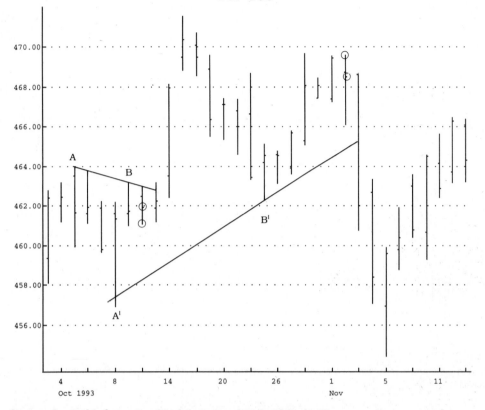

S&P 500

Source: Logical Information Machines, Inc. (LIM), Chicago, IL.

Figure 1.43 By calculating the difference between the close on the day prior to an upside breakout and that same day's low (or the previous day's close, whichever is less) and adding that difference to the close prior to the breakout, validation of the breakout is determined. If the difference added to the close is less than the breakout price, a valid breakout is identified. If the difference is greater than the breakout price, a false breakout is likely to occur. Specifically, in this example, the difference between the close and the low on the day prior to the breakout above TD Supply Line A-B is calculated and it is less, thus qualifying the breakout. TD Demand Line A'-B' is also drawn, and the same concept in reverse qualifies the downside breakout (see Figure 1.45).

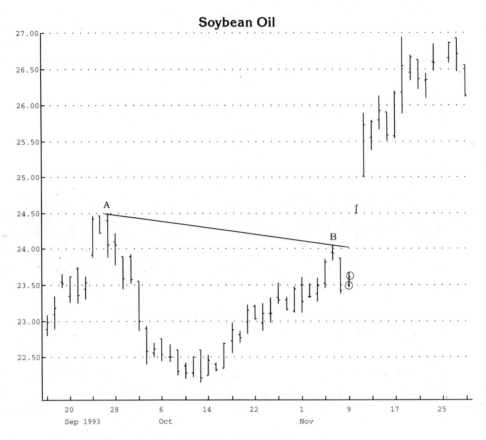

Source: Logical Information Machines, Inc. (LIM), Chicago, IL.

Figure 1.44   The difference between the close and the low on the day prior to the upside breakout of A-B Supply Line added to the close on the day prior to the breakout is less than the breakout price. Consequently, a valid breakout has been confirmed.

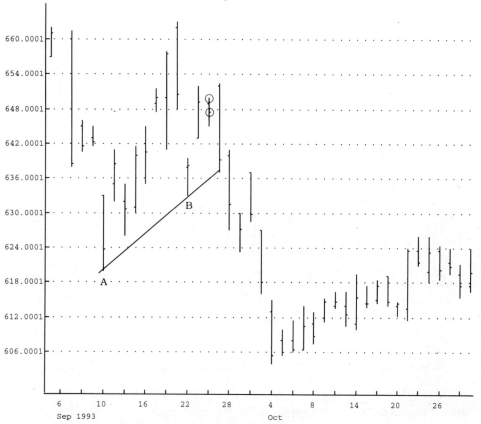

Soybeans

Source: Logical Information Machines, Inc. (LIM), Chicago, IL.

Figure 1.45   By subtracting the difference between the high one day before a downside breakout (or the close two days before it, if it is greater than the high one day before the breakout) and the close the day before the breakout from the close that same day, the breakout can be validated. In this instance, the A-B Demand Line was less and the breakout was validated.

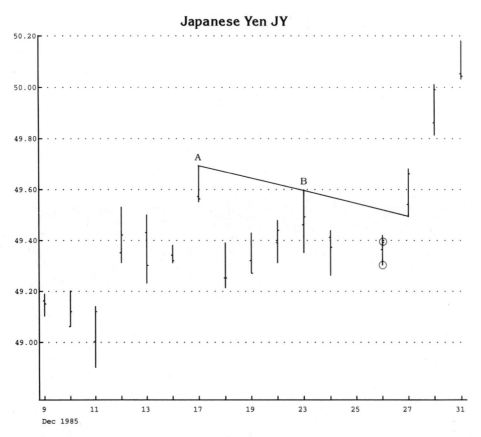

Source: Logical Information Machines, Inc. (LIM), Chicago, IL.

Figure 1.46   The difference between the close and the low the day before the breakout added to the breakout is less than the breakout price, thus validating the breakout.

Table 1.3   TD Breakout Qualifiers

TD Breakout Qualifier 1:

To validate a buy signal, the close the day before a buy signal is a down close. To validate a sell signal, the close the day before a sell signal is an up close.

TD Breakout Qualifier 2:

To validate a buy signal, a price open greater than the breakout price must occur. To validate a sell signal, a price open less than the breakout price must occur.

TD Breakout Qualifier 3:

To validate a buy signal, the value arrived at by adding the difference between the close and the low the day prior to a breakout or the close 2 days before whichever is less to that same day's close must be less than the breakout price. To validate a sell signal, the value arrived at by subtracting the difference between the high or the close 2 days before whichever is greater and the close the day prior to a breakout from that same day's close must be greater than the breakout price.

Chapter

Retracements

Price advances and declines do not continue uninterrupted. Contra-trend rallies and trend reversals occur all the time. Predicting the extent and the duration of these moves is a preoccupation of market analysts. Techniques to project these retracement levels, however, are not only inexact but also often haphazardly applied. Generally, little preparation and forethought are given to the selection of the points critical to the calculation of both support and resistance levels. Through trial and error, I have identified proper price selection techniques, as well as ratios, that can be universally applied to all markets. I have replaced the practice of random selection and guesswork with an objective, mechanical approach that offers a series of explanations and includes examples to justify my techniques.

Selection of Points and Retracement Ratios

In the summer of 1973, one of my senior business associates gave a compelling speech forecasting a steep retracement rally for the stock market to be completed by early fall. When quizzed regarding the upside potential, he flatly stated that he expected an advance approximating three-eighths to five-eighths of the previous decline. When asked to be more precise, he was unable to do so. When asked how he arrived at these figures, he flippantly responded that most rallies in a bear market expire at one of these two levels. He could not supply any additional information other than the fact that he had read of similar ratios in a market letter and suggested I contact the writer to learn of the significance and origin of these numbers. When I called, the writer made reference to a market analyst by the name of R. N. Elliott and an article he had written in *Financial World* many years earlier. At the library, I was able to retrieve the article from the archives. What I read regarding Fibonacci numbers was fascinating and informative. Unfortunately, it proved to be woefully incomplete. I began an exhaustive examination of price activity to uncover a precise, objective approach to calculating retracements. My goal was to identify a method that was mechanical and had application to all markets. The conclusions of my research are presented in the following discussion.

Rather than devote a lengthy amount of time and space to a discussion of Fibonacci numbers and their presence and dominance in nature and in surroundings, I recommend, should you desire further information, that you consult the numerous recent textbooks and articles dealing with the subject matter and the "golden mean." Briefly, I highlight the significance of the Fibonacci time series starting with the numbers 1, 2, 3, 5, 8, 13, 21, 34, 55, . . . and so on. Essentially, these numbers are obtained by summing two consecutive numbers in the series to arrive at the next number. As the numbers increase in size, the ratio obtained by dividing a preceding number by a succeeding number approaches .618, and, conversely, the ratio obtained by dividing a succeeding number by a preceding number is 1.618. This is a characteristic peculiar only to this specific time series.

I apply these numbers and ratios to much of my work. Specifically, in the case of retracements, I use what has become the standard, the "mother of all retracement ratios": .618. I believe that in the early

1970s I was the first to apply .382 (1.00 − .618) retracements as well. The retracements increase from
.382 and .618 to unity or "magnet price" (not 1.00, as
most believe, but the high/low day's close, depending
on whether the correction is up or down). From the full
retracement to the magnet price, they continue 1.382,
1.618, and 2.236 (1.618 + .618), and in the case of a
market recording all-time, record highs, the actual ratios .618 and .382 times the absolute price high. The
series of retracement levels are described below (see
Table 2.1).

More important than the ratios themselves is the
selection of the price points required to calculate the
retracements. For most analysts, such a process is a
moving target. Once again, in order to maintain consistency and uniformity, I refined and defined these
price levels precisely and objectively. My research suggested that the best results were obtained by applying
the following procedures.

Assume a recent low has been recorded. To establish reference points for retracement price objectives,
extend an imaginary horizontal line from that recent
low toward the left side of the chart to the last time a
lower low had been recorded (see Figure 2.1). Next,
refer to the highest price between these two points;
that is the "critical price." By subtracting the recent
low from that value, price retracement levels can be
projected (see Figure 2.1). Conversely, to arrive at

Table 2.1   Retracement Factors

.382
.618
Magnet price (high/low day's close)
1.382
1.618
2.236
2.618
3.618

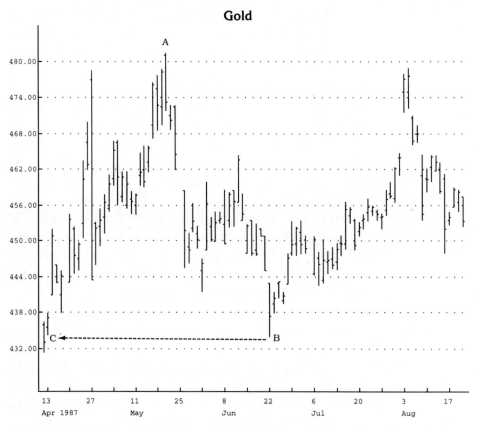

Gold

Source: Logical Information Machines, Inc. (LIM), Chicago, IL.

Figure 2.1 Once price level B has been defined, refer, on the left side of the chart, to the last time a lower low than that registered on day B was recorded (see price C). The highest high between these two points (A) is the critical price and is an important reference level when calculating upside retracements. By calculating the price difference between points A and B and multiplying by retracement factors, upside projections can be made. Notice how price hit an important obstacle at point A's close and not at the intraday high (refer to the discussion regarding magnet price and to Figure 2.5).

retracement levels off a price peak, the same exercise is performed in reverse. Specifically, extend an imaginary line from the recent price high toward the left side of the chart to the last time a higher high was made (see Figure 2.2). Identify the lowest low between these two points; that is the critical price. By subtracting the critical price from the recent high, price retracement levels can be projected (see Figure 2.2). Not only is this approach simple but it ensures that the

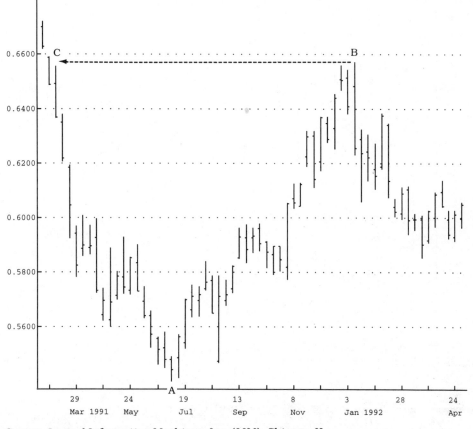

German mark (weekly)

Source: Logical Information Machines, Inc. (LIM), Chicago, IL.

Figure 2.2   To calculate the downside retracement levels, extend an imaginary line toward the left side of the chart to the last time a price high exceeded the high of point B (see price C). The lowest low between these two points (A) is the critical price and a key level when calculating downside retracements. By calculating the price difference between points A and B and multiplying by retracement factors, downside price projections can be made.

calculation of retracements will always be clear, well-defined, and uniform.

Experience has proven that the initial retracement levels of .382 and .618 are valid and predictable when the critical price point is properly identified (see Figures 2.3 and 2.4). However, most analysts who had even accidentally selected the correct points were mistaken when they assumed that, once price had exceeded both the .382 and .618 levels, the next

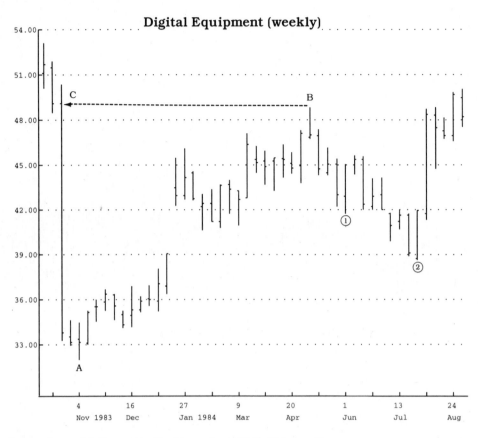

Source: Logical Information Machines, Inc. (LIM), Chicago, IL.

Figure 2.3 By identifying the lowest low between points B and C—the recent high (B) and the last time a higher high was recorded (C)—downside retracement levels can be calculated. Marked on the chart are levels 1 and 2, which identify .382 and .618 retracements of the move from point A to point B.

objective was the critical price day's high in the case of a rally and the critical price day's low in the case of a decline. In actuality, this widespread expectation has served for years as merely a decoy for unsuspecting traders (see Figure 2.5). My research with retracements many years ago uncovered a more crucial level, which served as a resistance/support level. Consequently, I refer to this price as the "magnet price." How often have you awaited penetration of a critical price high/low to liquidate or to enter a trade, only to witness price reverse direction early without a fill? In other instances, it is not uncommon to see price

United Airlines (weekly)

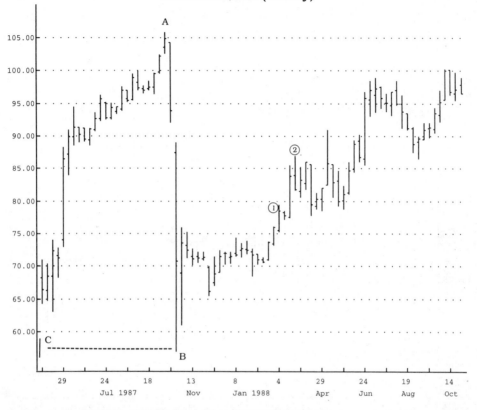

Source: Logical Information Machines, Inc. (LIM), Chicago, IL.

Figure 2.4   By identifying the highest high between points B and C—the recent low (B) and the last time a lower low was recorded (C)—upside retracement levels can be calculated. Marked on the chart are levels 1 and 2, which correspond with .382 and .618 retracement levels of the move from point A to point B.

accelerate through a critical price and immediately proceed to the 1.382 level, just at the time when everyone expects support at the intraday low or resistance at the intraday high. Unexpected movements occur at this price level when one is not properly prepared.

There are exceptions to the retracement calculations presented above. Experience suggests that the previous examples are associated with trading range markets. Once price advances to record all-time highs, however, the selection of a "critical point" (low)

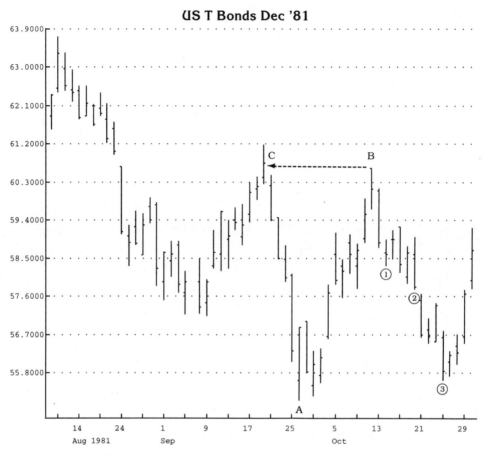

US T Bonds Dec '81

Source: Logical Information Machines, Inc. (LIM), Chicago, IL.

Figure 2.5 Observe how price retraced to levels 1 and 2 and eventually declined to the low day's range exceeding that day's close. How many traders were expecting a test of the low price at point A and were fooled? The key is the "magnet price"—low day's close.

is impossible, because no other high exists farther left on the chart. In these instances, I have found multiplying the absolute peak price by .618 and by .382 works well. Two instances are indelibly etched upon my memory. The first is a forecast I made to an audience in New York prior to the 1987 stock market crash. At that time, the August price high for the Dow Jones Industrial Average was approximately 2747—a record. By multiplying that value by .618, I was able to calculate a support (retracement) level for

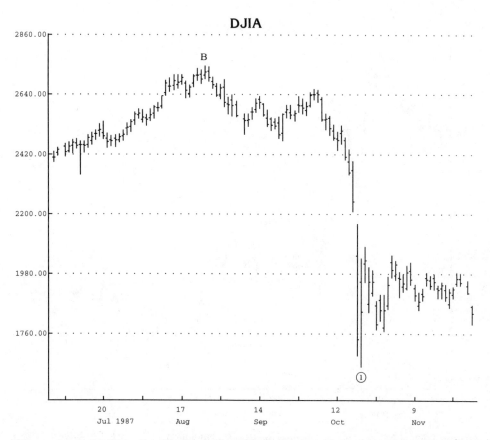

Source: Logical Information Machines, Inc. (LIM), Chicago, IL.

Figure 2.6(a)   If one were to extend an imaginary line from point B to the last time price recorded a higher high to identify a reference low in between, he would be unable, because price had never been higher. In these rare instances, valid downside price projections can be calculated by merely multiplying the absolute high by .618 and by .382. In this example, price met good support at level 1, which approximates .618 times the high.

the market of approximately 1697 (see Figure 2.6a). I presented that level to the audience as my downside price projection. At the same time, I presented a TD Line breakout objective of 1650 (see the trendline discussion in Chapter 1). Although mechanically and objectively derived in both instances, it was surprising how both reinforced one another and lent credibility and conviction to my forecast.

Another episode involving the application of this retracement approach relates to a forecast I made

Nikkei weekly

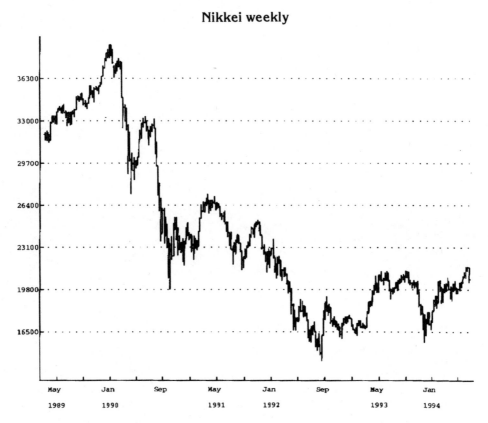

Source: Logical Information Machines, Inc. (LIM), Chicago, IL.

Figure 2.6(b) Using the DeMark technique to predict the downside price objective.

subsequent to the Nikkei Average recording its all-time high at 38957. I had been sponsored by a large brokerage house and was invited to make a series of speeches in Japan regarding various Japanese markets. Invariably, the topic would be directed to the Japanese stock market. Due to the fact that a record high had been realized and that no "critical price" (low) could be identified, I applied my approach to the Nikkei Average. As you can see on Figure 2.6b, the technique accurately predicted the downside price objective below 15,000. At the time the forecast was made, skepticism and ridicule were common. Once price had accomplished this downside objective, however, respect for the technique was pervasive.

TD Retracement Arcs

Another method I developed many years ago projects retracement levels incorporating both price and time. I had never seen anything quite like it prior to my research and have never seen anything similar since. Instead of identifying one retracement price objective as most other techniques do, this approach has a

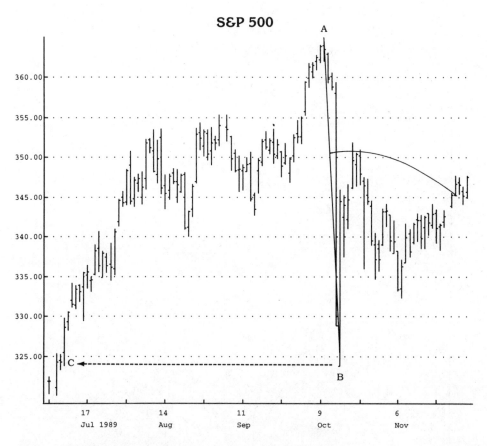

Source: Logical Information Machines, Inc. (LIM), Chicago, IL.

Figure 2.7   This unique approach incorporates both price and time. The reference points are identified the same as before, but once identified the two points are connected with a straight-edge ruler and the retracement levels (.382, .618, and the magnet price) are identified on this line. Then, by using point B as a fulcrum, an arc is extended to the right of the chart; once a price close exceeds the arc in the future, it proceeds to the next TD Retracement Arc level. This assumes that the points are properly anchored to avoid any changes in the shape in the arc when either the price or the calendar scale is changed.

floating price objective that adjusts to the passage of time. More specifically, the price objective changes from day to day. The specific price resides on an arc.

The arc is constructed by drawing a line that connects the critical price and the recent low/high, depending on whether an advance or a decline is expected. Once the .382 and the .618 points on the line itself are identified, the recent low/high serves as a fulcrum or a pivot point for an arc that extends from those points into the future. The curve that appears describes retracement projections (see Figures 2.7 and 2.8). As price declines below/above the pivot point, a new arc must be drawn.

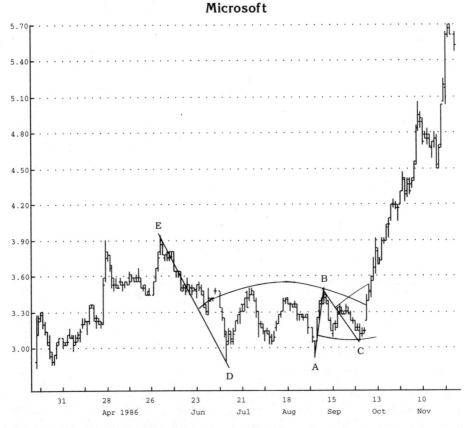

Microsoft

Source: Logical Information Machines, Inc. (LIM), Chicago, IL.

Figure 2.8 Note the numerous TD Retracement Arcs formed by lines extending from points B-A, C-B, and D-E. The arc formed by B-A is reversed by the arc defined by C-B, and the price breakout upside above the latter arc is confirmed by a similar breakout above the larger TD Retracement Arc D-E.

Retracement Qualifiers

Important elements of my TD Lines are the TD Breakout Qualifiers (see the discussion of TD Line in Chapter
1). They are extraordinary filters that predetermine
whether an intraday breakout is valid or invalid. So
too, moves exceeding .382 and .618 retracements can
be prescreened as legitimate or not. My research suggests that these same TD Breakout Qualifiers apply

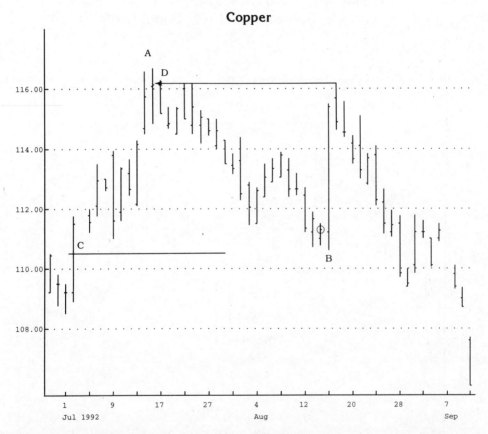

Source: Logical Information Machines, Inc. (LIM), Chicago, IL.

Figure 2.9   The close on the day before point B is a down close (circled),
which satisfies TD Retracement Qualifier 1, indicates an oversold condition,
and improves the prospects for intraday entry and a successful trade to the
retracement levels. In this instance, the .382 and the .618 retracement levels
were fulfilled the same day. In fact, the move the following day extended to
the magnet price (D)—point A close—and did not, as most traders would expect, reach point A day's high.

equally well to validating retracements. To remain
consistent with the topic, however, I refer to these
qualifiers as TD Retracement Qualifiers 1, 2, and 3. It
might be worthwhile to reiterate their respective definitions. Specifically, TD Retracement Qualifier 1 requires that the close on the day prior to an advance
above the retracement level be down in order to qualify
for intraday entry and the expectation that the advance will continue (see Figure 2.9). Conversely, it provides that the close on the day before a decline below
the retracement level be up in order to qualify for intraday entry and the expectation that the decline will
continue (see Figure 2.10). Should this qualifier in

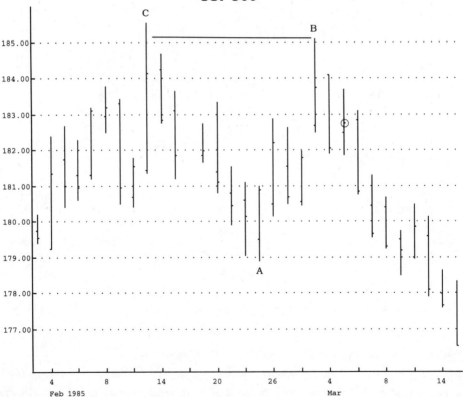

Source: Logical Information Machines, Inc. (LIM), Chicago, IL.

Figure 2.10   The close the day before the .618 retracement level was an up
close (circled) and implied a valid retracement, as well as justified intraday
entry. TD Retracement Qualifier 1 has been satisfied.

either situation be lacking, the potential of the advance or the decline reversing, rather than accelerating, at those precise points increases significantly. Another possibility exists, and that is TD Retracement Qualifier 2. In this instance, both an upside and a downside penetration can qualify, provided price exceeds the retracement level on the opening (see Figures 2.11 and 2.12). This occurrence suggests that the price dynamics are so strong that entry is validated and that the continuation of the move is imminent. One additional qualifier (TD Qualifier 3) can be incorporated into one's trading arsenal. The concept

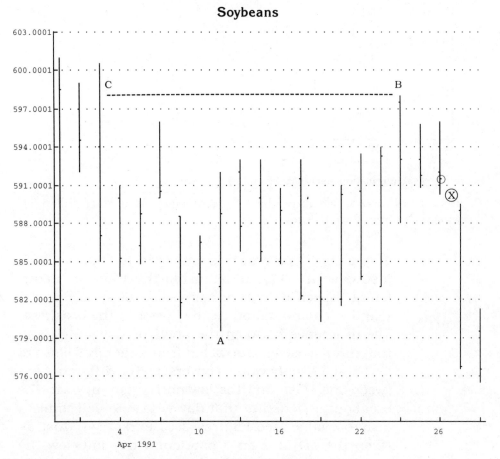

Source: Logical Information Machines, Inc. (LIM), Chicago, IL.

Figure 2.11   See the opening gap downside (X) below the .382 retracement level. This fulfills the requirement of TD Retracement Qualifier 2 and negates the fact that the previous day's close was a down close (see circled close).

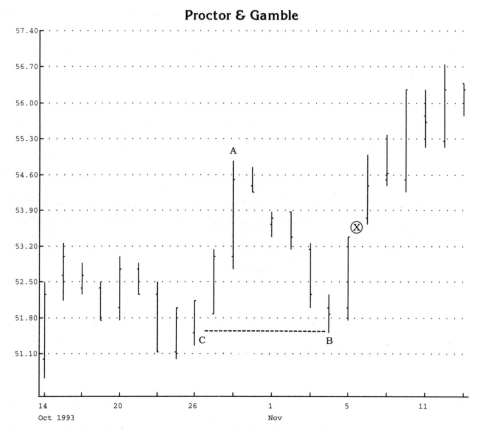

Proctor & Gamble

Source: Logical Information Machines, Inc. (LIM), Chicago, IL.

Figure 2.12   Price gapped above the .618 retracement level and fulfilled Retracement Qualifier 2 in the process.

of overbought/oversold is employed in this instance just as with TD Qualifier 1, but the approach is different. Specifically, the expression of supply or demand is calculated on the day prior to the breakout. The difference between the previous day's high and that day's close is subtracted from that day's close to arrive at a supply value; conversely, the difference between the close and the low on the day prior to the breakout is added to that day's close to determine a demand value (see Figures 2.13 and 2.14). Just as when the TD Line on a particular day is below the supply value or above the demand value and a legitimate breakout is recorded by price exceeding the TD Line, so too the same approach applies to retracement points. In fact, in those exceptional instances when

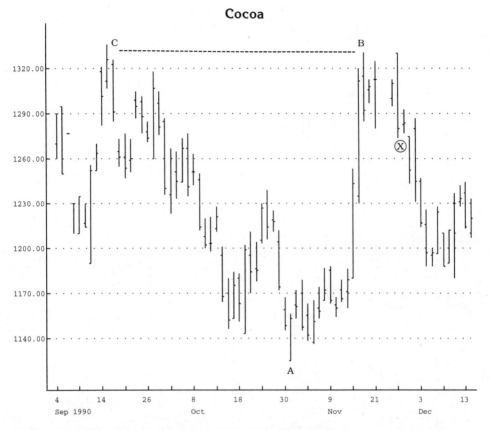

Source: Logical Information Machines, Inc. (LIM), Chicago, IL.

Figure 2.13 By calculating the difference between the high the day before penetration of a retracement level (or the close the previous day, whichever is greater) and the close the day before the breakout, and subtracting that value from that close and then comparing it with the retracement level, it can be determined whether price will continue to the next lower retracement level or reverse. If the retracement price is below the value, then price should continue to decline; if the retracement price is above that value, then price should attempt to rally. The difference between the high and the close the day before X retracement level is above the .382 retracement point; consequently, price continued to decline. TD Qualifier 3 has been fulfilled.

both the TD Line and the retracement levels are qualified, they appear to reinforce one another and translate into successful trades.

As displayed in Table 2.1, there exists a series of retracement levels; when one is exceeded, price gravitates typically toward the next level. Not included in Table 2.1 nor in the earlier discussion, however, is a

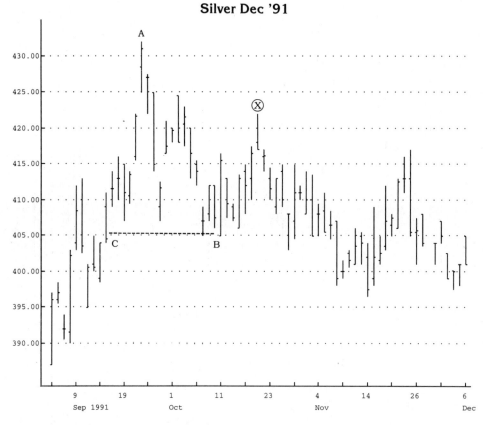

Source: Logical Information Machines, Inc. (LIM), Chicago, IL.

Figure 2.14 Price failed at the retracement level because the difference between the previous day's close and low added to that same day's close was greater than the retracement level.

hybrid situation that refines retracement expectations even further. Despite the fact that price may exceed a retracement level and that a retracement qualifier may have been satisfied, a situation may arise in which the closing price is unable to remain in excess of the retracement value. Provided that the closing price does not fail to exceed the previous day's close, the only adjustment required is a minor one. Instead of the next retracement level being the one listed in Table 2.1, it is actually one-half of the distance between the two levels. For example, if price exceeds the .382 retracement level, is properly qualified, and closes above the previous day's close but fails to close above the .382 retracement level, the expectation level is no longer a .618 retracement objective; rather it is the 50 percent level. Furthermore, should all prerequisites be satisfied at the .618 level but the closing price fail, the revised retracement level would be one-half the distance from .618 to the critical price or the magnet price, whichever is less. The same process occurs, in reverse, when price declines.

A final variation of retracements incorporates both price and time, as does the TD Retracement Arc. Rather than identify on an arc the time and the price retracement level, this approach applies a meter to the amount of time allotted to accomplish penetration of the retracement level. For example, if the number of days from a peak to a low is counted and this value is multiplied by .382, an expiration time in which to fulfill a retracement is defined. The same concept can be applied to larger retracements, such as .618.

During the mid-1970s, in order to simplify the process of calculating price retracements, I purchased a proportional divider. I ordered this device from Teledyne-Post and it had to be sent from overseas. Since that time, I have shared this tool with many other market analysts and subsequently they have purchased their own. I recommend that if you work with price charts and if you quickly want to approximate retracement levels, then purchase one from your local art or drafting supply store.

The discussion above describes methods to objectively define the parameters for calculating and qualifying retracements. The beauty of these approaches is that they are totally objective. No allowance for subjective interference or for personal bias is permitted. In the final analysis, no excuses can be attributed to faulty suppositions. Everything considered is hard and fast, with clearly defined rules for application and interpretation.

Trend Factors™

Often, both traders and investors preoccupy themselves with market rhetoric. As far as I am concerned, however, one distinction they fail to recognize or to acknowledge is the difference between the duration and the degree of price moves. Invariably, were I to ask for definitions to widely used market terms such as short, intermediate, and long term, I would wager that most, if not all, would respond in temporal terms. Although the responses might vary somewhat, I would expect to hear that short term relates to moves of less than one month's duration, intermediate term to moves longer than one month but shorter than six months, and long term to moves lasting more than six months. These labels may have been appropriate prior to the 1980s, but because of increased volatility in the financial markets, they have become outdated. Moves that in the past consumed weeks or months are being fulfilled in days or hours. Because of market illiquidity, the speed of news dissemination, the herd instinct of fund managers, and other factors, this trend continues. Consequently, I apply the descriptions of short, intermediate, and long term to percentage price movements rather than to specific time intervals. For example, I consider moves of less than 5 percent to be short term, moves of 5 to 15 percent to be intermediate term, and moves greater than 15 percent to be long term. These definitions apply regardless of the time required to accomplish these moves. In this context, I rely on an analytical tool I developed many years ago to forecast the inception of trend moves of an intermediate to long-term variety. I refer to the set of specific ratios I use as Trend Factors™.

In the early 1970s, I observed a dominant tendency for various markets to exhibit support and resistance at price intervals defined by percentage retracements from preceding price peaks and troughs. For example, upside resistance levels were projected by multiplying a recent low by a series of prescribed ratios. Conversely, downside support levels were calculated by multiplying a recent price peak by the inverse of the upside ratios. Through a tedious trial-and-error process, I was able to approximate the ideal ratio values. I established prerequisites to qualify the reference highs and lows and to ensure consistency and uniformity. The selection criteria necessary to identify the correct reference value—whether high, low, or close—were critical to defining the price trend and the anticipated price movement.

In order to define it, a reference low must first be qualified. Because the minimum Trend Factor ratio is .0556, a qualified low exists once price has declined to a value at most .9444 from a previous qualified reference high day's close (see Figure 2.15). Conversely, a qualified high exists once price has advanced the minimum Trend Factor 1.0556 from a previous qualified reference low day's close (see Figure 2.16). It's that

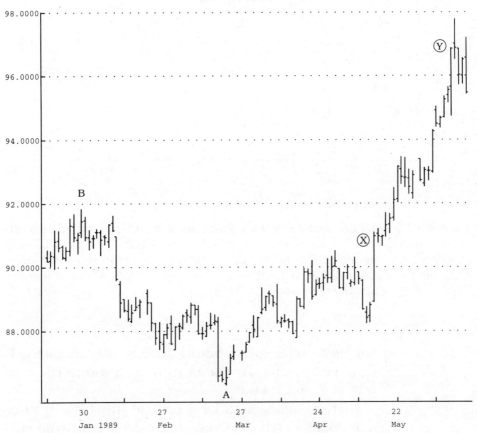

US T Bonds

Source: Logical Information Machines, Inc. (LIM), Chicago, IL.

Figure 2.15 From point B to point A, price declined more than .0556—in other words, the value of point A is no more than .9444 times the value of point A. This validates point A as a Trend Factor low. Price X is the 1.0556 level and price Y is the 1.112 level.

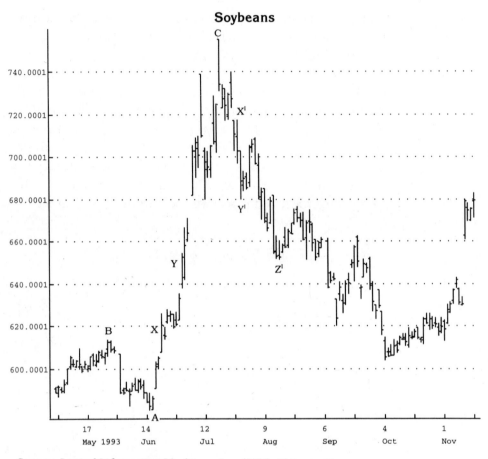

Source: Logical Information Machines, Inc. (LIM), Chicago, IL.

Figure 2.16   Point A is no more than .9444 point B and is qualified as a reference point. Price levels X and Y correspond to 1.0556 and 1.112 Trend Factor objectives. Point C qualifies as a Trend Factor high reference point because price advanced from point A by more than 1.0556. X' and Y' identify Trend Factor objectives, as does Z.

simple to select price points that qualify. Before getting too specific, I'd like to introduce you to the concept of Trend Factors™.

There appears to be a critical juncture in price movement, at which point, once price momentum surpasses on a closing basis key support or resistance levels, it is able to proceed to the next critical juncture. The market itself legitimizes those price moves. An alert trader can capitalize on the message the price movement sends once it exceeds these critical price levels. Figures 2.15 and 2.16 demonstrate this phenomenon. As identified earlier, the essential ingredients are the qualification and the selection of the reference point and then the Trend Factor ratios. To determine the first level of resistance upside, the reference point must be multiplied by 1.0056; to arrive at the second level of resistance upside, the reference point must be multiplied by 1.112 (2 × .0556); and to calculate the third level of resistance, the reference point must be multiplied by 1.14 ($2^1/_2$ × .0556). On the other hand, to determine the first level of support downside, the reference point must be multiplied by .9444; to arrive at the second level of support downside, the first downside target must be multiplied by .9444 again (this is different from the upside process); and to calculate the third level of support downside, the second level must be multiplied by .9722 ($^1/_2$ of value between .9444 and 1.000).

It is important to select the proper reference price value, to ensure that the support and the resistance levels are defined accurately. My research has confirmed that specific patterns identify what price to use to calculate these threshold levels. Specifically, if (1) the reference day's close is less than the close one day earlier, and (2) the close one day before the reference day's close is less than the close two days earlier, and (3) the close one day after the reference day's low is greater than the reference day's close, then the upside resistance level and projection values are determined by multiplying the reference day's low by the ratios. If either the reference day's close or the close one day before is an up close or an unchanged close, then the reference price used to calculate the first resistance level is the reference day's close. The only exception arises when the low the day after the reference day exceeds the close of the reference day. In this instance, the first level of resistance is determined by multiplying the close on that day by the ratio 1.0556 (see Figure 2.17). The second and third levels of resistance are calculated by using the reference day's low.

When defining the first level of support, as well as the next two levels of downside price projections, a

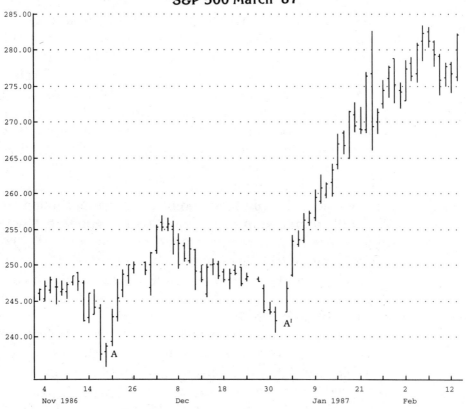

S&P 500 March '87

Source: Logical Information Machines, Inc. (LIM), Chicago, IL.

Figure 2.17   A and A' identify days after reference lows in which price gaps exist—the low fails to intersect the previous day's close. Consequently, the Trend Factors are multiplied by the closes on these days.

similar evaluation of closing price relationships must be done. If the close of the reference day as well as the day prior to the reference day are up closes, then the high of the reference day is used to project the critical support level and the second support level is projected by multiplying the first support level by .9444. The third support level is .9722 times the second. If either the close the day before the reference day or the close the day of the reference day is a down close, then the same ratio is multiplied by the reference day's close. The only exception arises when the high the day after the reference day is less than the reference day's close. In this instance, the first level of support is deter-

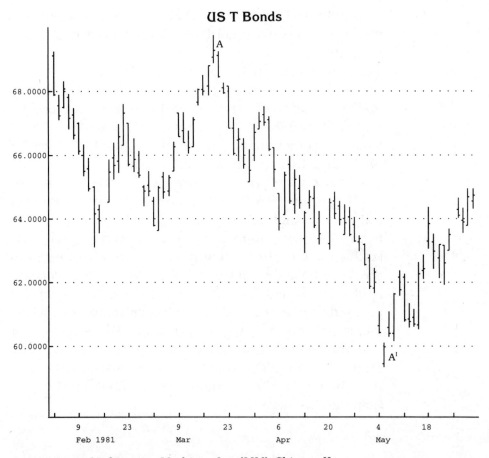

US T Bonds

Source: Logical Information Machines, Inc. (LIM), Chicago, IL.

Figure 2.18 A identifies a day on which the high does not intersect the previous day's close and, consequently, a price gap exists. The Trend Factor is multiplied by the close on that specific day. A' identifies a reference low defined by an upside gap.

mined by multiplying the close that day by the factor .9444 (see Figure 2.18). The second and third levels of support are calculated by using the reference day's high.

Generally, the first attempt to exceed level one, established by the low or the high multiplied by the Trend Factor, is accomplished easily. However, in those instances where price exceeds the projection and closes in the direction of the trend but fails to close above or below it, the next trend factor objective is reduced by 50 percent—specifically, level two price projection is 1.0834 and .9722. These exceptions apply only when price confirms level one intraday but not on a close.

One exception to those rules does exist. Due to the fact that some futures' markets are quoted in decimals such as the currencies, and are not preceded by any whole numbers, it is important to adjust the Trend Factor™, to include another prefix—.99444 instead of .9444 and 1.00556 instead of 1.0556.

I have found that the support and the resistance levels projected by utilizing Trend Factors™ are often uncannily exact (see Figure 2.18). It is not uncommon to witness price approach a level or even exceed it intraday, only to then fail and reverse trend at precisely the Trend Factor™ level. Conversely, once a defined level is exceeded on a closing basis, price generally proceeds to the next level. The keys to success when using this approach revolve around the selection of reference points and the proper implementation of the Trend Factors™. The same filters discussed earlier in this chapter can be applied equally well to qualify anticipated breakouts.

Chapter

Overbought/Oversold

Most market analysts use indicators to identify zones of high-risk or low-risk buying opportunity. They label these areas as either over-bought or oversold. Typically, they associate overbought readings with selling and oversold readings with buying. Unfortunately, such classifications are more misleading than helpful. Once again, most seemingly intelligent and rational investors overlook numer-ous unprofitable signals and do not conduct the research required for explanations of why they failed. For years, this had bothered me.

It was never my nature to ignore or to dismiss the numerous shortcomings and failures of a market timing approach. I could have speculated why the interpretations assigned to the buy/sell zones were invalid or lacking, but I wanted substantive evidence and I pur-sued it relentlessly. Unfortunately, there exists no stronger incen-tive for involvement than to be engaged in a personal trade that quickly becomes unprofitable. My experience trading suggests a strong correlation between actively being involved—trading your personal account and applying techniques—and passively being in-volved—perusing a chart and making hypothetical trades. Every unprofitable price tick in your personal account seems to inspire more determination to uncover a decision rule that would prevent similar uncomfortable situations in the future. Through a process

of trial and error over 15 years ago, I was able to uncover a set of rules to follow when interpreting indicators. The conclusions of my research are presented in
this chapter.

Most commonly used indicators, such as RSI or
stochastics, are followed religiously by their disci-
ples. These individuals accept as doctrine the widely
followed rules and interpretations assigned to these
indicator values. It's surprising, however, just how
little research they conduct themselves before they
install such indicators into their trading regimen.
Substantial amounts of money are placed at risk, yet
little effort is expended to perform the minimum due
diligence required to establish the indicators' efficacy.
I'd like to share with you an incident I witnessed a
number of years ago to substantiate this claim.

With the introduction of computers and market
software in the late 1970s, it was not uncommon to
see market analysts pore over short-term price movements and indicator gyrations. I observed one such individual in action and could not believe my eyes—it
was an exercise in futility and foolishness. If it hadn't
been so sad, it would have been great comedy. As is the
case with most traders who use "canned program" indicators, this individual had no clue whatsoever of the
composition of the indicator he was following. All he
knew was that it appeared to work well historically. He
should have known that that excuse alone was an invitation to trading suicide. As with most indicators, the
entries on a chart are recorded after a particular time
period has lapsed. The various movements that take
place within the time period do not appear on the
chart. As you might have expected, this individual
was trapped in a game of indicator "false starts."
What I am suggesting is that camouflaged between
two indicator entries are often moves that generate
signals but then disappear by the time the official entry period is completed.

Within a 30-minute period, this individual entered a particular trade three times and exited all three
at a loss. Unfortunately, with this pattern of trading,
no one benefited but his broker. Such a situation is not

unusual, once a trader becomes convinced he can easily realize success and wealth without doing his homework. I admonished this individual that to acquire a better understanding of and an appreciation for the construction and intricacies of the indicator he used required an effort on his part. Had he conducted such an exercise, he would have been aware of the vagaries and nuances of the indicator, as well as the fact that bogus intraperiod signals were inherent to the indicator. I recommended to him that, in order to get an accurate assessment of the indicator's value, he should (1) concentrate on the closing price, which coincided with the completion of the indicator time frame, to determine his true entry price, and (2) ignore ranges because a chart displaying daily highs and lows gives a false perspective of reality. My pursuit to prevent situations such as these resulted in my examination of the most widely followed indicators, as well as the creation of my own stable of indicators. The following discussion highlights what I have found to be the proper interpretation of most indicator-driven overbought/oversold readings.

Proper Interpretation: Mild versus Severe

In August 1982, the stock market recorded a low of major proportions. Soon afterward, the market exploded upside with unprecedented power and thrust. All widely followed price indicators immediately swung from mildly oversold levels to an extreme of severely overbought. As I expected at the time, the consensus of market followers was that, because of this excessive overbought condition, the market would experience a price decline. This never occurred (see Figure 3.1). Just as a rocket requires excessive thrust to be launched out of the earth's atmosphere and into orbit, so too, should the market enjoy a similar experience, a comparable fate would arise: the law of market gravity would at least temporarily be repealed. Observation and experience have proven that market

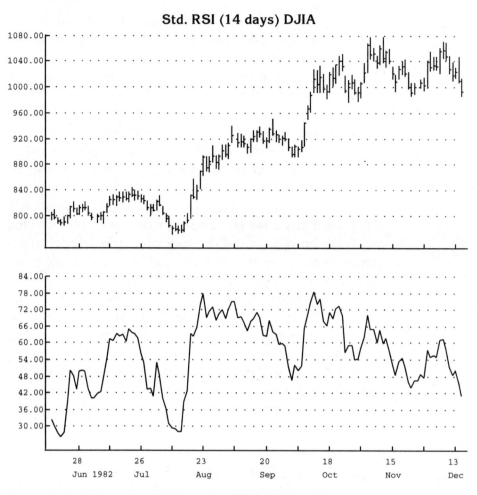

Std. RSI (14 days) DJIA

Source: Logical Information Machines, Inc. (LIM), Chicago, IL.

Figure 3.1 The 14-day RSI indicator remained in overbought territory—above 65—for an extended period of time throughout August, as well as in October. These extended periods of overbought are not selling opportunities; rather, they are times to step aside or even enter trades because the demand is so excessive that it first must dissipate (recycle) and then move into overbought and record a mild, not excessive, reading.

conditions such as these are extraordinary. In this case, for example, an excessive overbought state would not translate into a high-risk buy situation or into a selling opportunity, but rather into an exceptional buying opportunity because of the stampede nature of the advance. The extreme sense of urgency to buy is not associated with a price peak. Generally, the previously defined supply–demand equilibrium level is so disrupted by this surge in demand that it takes a considerable amount of time to dissipate. In fact, I discovered some time ago that such imbalances had similar characteristics.

Through extensive research, I realized that there were instances of overbought and of oversold conditions that translated into price reversals. I identified a common denominator related to these cases. Specifically, mild overbought/oversold readings correlate well with price turning points. On the other hand, extreme or excessive overbought/oversold readings do not conform and consequently vex most analysts. My work suggested that all that was required was a "recycling" out of the excessive mode back into a neutral zone, and then a second—or third, if necessary—attempt to record a mild reading as a prelude to a price reversal (see Figure 3.2).

My conclusions regarding the proper interpretation of overbought/oversold contradict what most other analysts teach and believe. Specifically, in order to reconcile the fact that the messages sent by their indicators are often premature, most analysts tend to rely on a type of analysis referred to within the market timing industry as divergence analysis. In actuality, this approach misses the point entirely; it is merely the symptom, not the cause. Let me explain. Time is the crucial determinant, whether the condition is labeled mild or extreme. The degree or extent of overbought/oversold is incidental and secondary. Through trial and error, I concluded that, generally, if an indicator is rated overbought/oversold for a period of five or fewer days (other units of time may be substituted as well), the rating is mild. On the other hand, if an indicator is rated overbought/oversold for more than five days, the rating is extreme. As you can see, the key variable is duration (see Figure 3.3).

There does exist a rare instance when an indicator records almost the most extreme possible reading for an extended period of time. The implications are then identical to those of a mild reading, and the expectation is for a reversal (see Figure 3.4). In such an instance, the indicator is positioned at a level that corresponds to such an extreme that it appears to be off the chart.

Std. RSI (14 days) US T Bonds

Source: Logical Information Machines, Inc. (LIM), Chicago, IL.

Figure 3.2   The readings of overbought—above 65—were for extended periods in July and August and for a short period of time in September.

Overall Market Environment

Other techniques can be employed to complement and enhance the performance of this approach of indicator evaluation and interpretation. Specifically, I recommend strongly that a longer-term wave perspective of price activity be followed as well, in order to serve as an overlay defining the market's direction. In other words, once the environment is identified, only accept trades that are in concert with that trend. For example, if the

Std. RSI (14 days) Digital Equipment

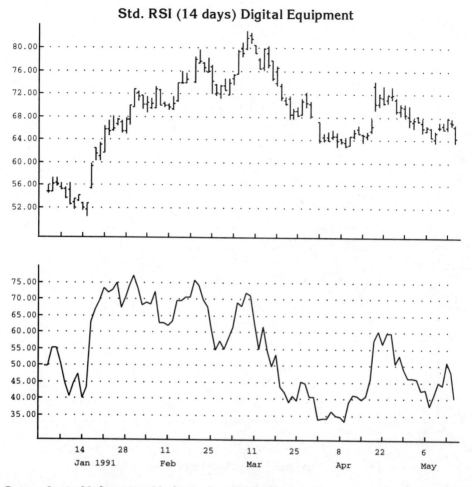

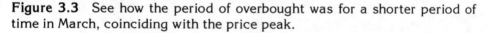

Source: Logical Information Machines, Inc. (LIM), Chicago, IL.

Figure 3.3   See how the period of overbought was for a shorter period of time in March, coinciding with the price peak.

trend is up and the current indicator reading is mildly oversold, action can be taken. Conversely, if the trend is down and the current indicator reading is mildly overbought, action can be taken. Otherwise, if they should contradict one another, postpone initiating any activity.

My experience has been that the delineation between mild and severe overbought/oversold is a key factor overlooked by most analysts. I attribute this oversight to a lack of both research ambition and creativity. However, it is not my intention to represent that my procedure is superior to all others by any

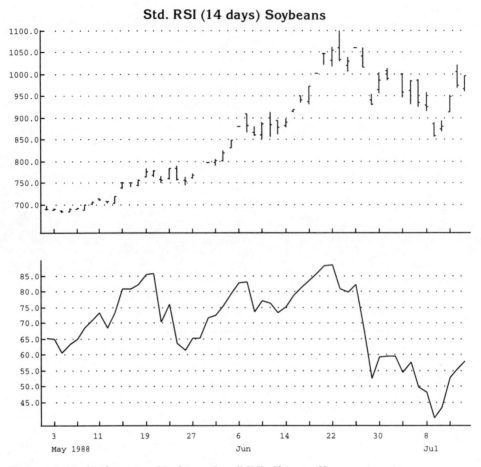

Std. RSI (14 days) Soybeans

Source: Logical Information Machines, Inc. (LIM), Chicago, IL.

Figure 3.4   The number of days in overbought was for such a long period of time that demand finally exhausted itself. This is an exception to the general rule.

means. It's just a perspective on indicator interpretation that is original and universally applicable.

Range Expansion Index (REI) and DeMarker Indicator

I introduce here two indicators that I created and have used for some time: (1) the Range Expansion Index (REI) and (2) the DeMarker Indicator. I offer both as alternatives to the many widely followed publicly traded indicators—a number of which, incidentally, I also developed.

The REI and the DeMarker have been designed to identify price exhaustion areas that generally correspond with price peaks and troughs. The aforementioned discussion regarding the proper interpretation of overbought/oversold readings applies to these indicators as well, but because these indicators are arithmetically and not exponentially calculated, the likelihood of extended extreme levels being realized is diminished. Furthermore, the time period used for the REI is 8 days, and severe or excessive readings hardly ever appear and then only for a limited time. The formulas and the rationale for the REI and the DeMarker Indicator are presented below.

Range Expansion Index (REI)

I have always been suspicious of the indicators commonly used by traders. I believed that universal usage and acceptance effectively canceled the benefits that could be derived from any of them. Consequently, either I improved on these indicators or created my own. One such indicator is the Range Expansion Index (REI). I wanted an indicator that was sensitive to periods of ascending *and* of descending prices but was silent during sideways price movement as well as during steep advances and declines. To accomplish this goal, I established the following guidelines. I compare the high and the low on a particular day with the high and the low two days before it. If the high price is higher than the high two days earlier, then a positive difference is recorded; if it is less than the high two days earlier, then a negative difference is recorded. If the low price is higher than the low two days earlier, then a positive difference is recorded; if it is less than the low two days earlier, then a negative value is recorded. Once these two values are calculated, they are summed together and a value is determined for that particular day.

Table 3.1 shows four possible relationships between today's price range activity versus the price range activity two days earlier. In relation to both the high and the low two days earlier:

1. Both today's high and low are greater;

2. Both are less than or equal to;

3. The high is greater and the low is less than or equal to;

4. The high is less than or equal to and the low is greater than or equal to.

By not comparing the current day with the previous day, short-term static is eliminated and there is greater assurance of a trending pattern. An additional condition requires that either the high two days earlier be greater than or equal to the close seven or eight days ago,

Table 3.1   Price Range Activity Comparison

Price high today is greater than price high two days ago

AND

Price low today is less than or equal to price low two days ago

OR

Price high today is less than or equal to price high two days ago

AND

Price low today is less than or equal to price low two days ago

OR

Price high today is greater than price high two days ago

AND

Price low today is greater than price low two days ago

OR

Price high today is less than or equal to price high two days ago

AND

Price low today is greater than price low two days ago

or the current high be greater than or equal to the low 5 or 6 days ago. This prevents buying into a steep decline by requiring price to exhibit some proof of slowing its decline. At the same time, either the low two days earlier must be less than or equal to the close seven or eight days ago, or the current low must be less than or equal to the low five or six days ago. Similarly, this ensures that the rate of advance is not excessive and helps prevent selling into blow-offs. In both these instances, a zero value is assigned if price action fails to confirm some slowdown in the rate of advance or decline. Over an eight-day period, all the positive and negative values are summed. The they are divided by the absolute value of the price movement, both positive and negative. An indicator (ratio) that fluctuates between 100 and −100 has been created.

My experience shows that, once the REI reading exceeds 60 and then declines below 60, price weakness should become apparent. Conversely, once the REI declines below −60 and then advances above −60, price strength should become apparent. The price charts in Figures 3.5 and 3.6 demonstrate this phenomenon. Included is the code prepared for the Logical Information Machine for the REI Macro, Table 3.2.

DeMarker Indicator

The DeMarker Indicator is constructed by making the following comparisons. The current day's high is compared with the high of the previous day. If the current high is higher, then the difference is determined and recorded. If, however, the current day's high is less than or equal to the previous day's high, then a zero is assigned and recorded. Then the daily differences are summed for a period of 13 days. This value becomes the numerator for the DeMarker Index and is divided by that same value plus the difference between the previous day's low and today's low, summed for a total of 13 days. If the current day's low is greater than the low one day ago, then a zero is assigned and recorded.

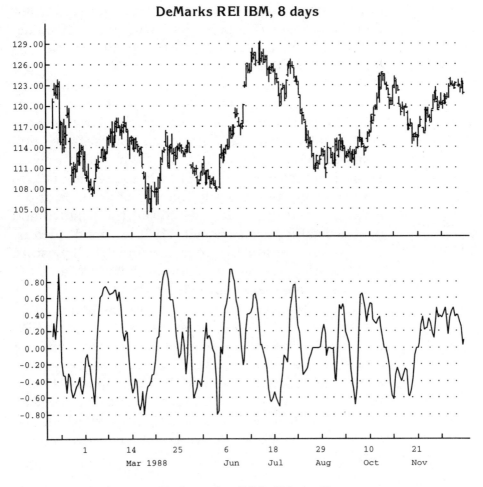

DeMarks REI IBM, 8 days

Source: Logical Information Machines, Inc. (LIM), Chicago, IL.

Figure 3.5 REI movement below −60 is generally associated with price lows. Conversely, REI movement above 60 is common at price peaks.

A simple indicator with sensitive and predicative properties has been created.

Figures 3.7 and 3.8 demonstrate this phenomenon clearly. As you can see, the indicator fluctuates between 0 and 100. Once the DeMarker Indicator declines below 30, a potential bottom has been identified. Conversely, once the indicator advances above 70, a potential top has been defined.

Just like the REI, the purpose of the DeMarker Indicator is to identify both high-risk and low-risk buy areas. Whereas the REI is designed to make price comparisons every other day to ensure proper trend

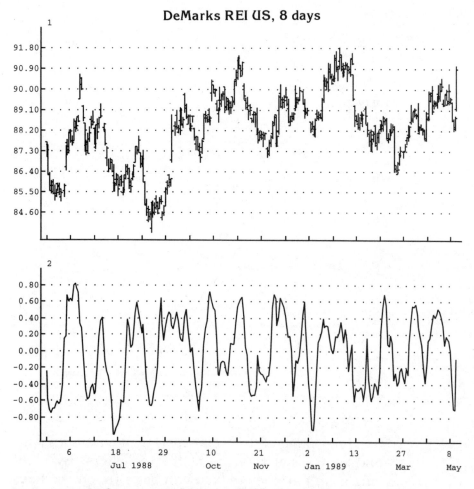

DeMarks REI US, 8 days

Source: Logical Information Machines, Inc. (LIM), Chicago, IL.

Figure 3.6   Both charts (Figures 3.5 and 3.6) depict the relationship between the movement of the Range Expansion Index (REI) and the price activity of the underlying security. Activity above 60 and below −60 generally coincides with price peaks and troughs. Specifically, once price crosses above −60 from below and once price crosses below 60 from above, indications of reversal are present.

identification, the DeMarker evaluates price movement from one day to the next. In addition, the REI is calculated over a 8-day period and the DeMarker is constructed using a 13-day average. (The time parameters for both indicators can be adjusted from the standard 8 and 13 days at any time.) Included is the code prepared for the Logical Information Machine for the DeMarker Indicator, Table 3.3.

Table 3.2   DeMarks REI 8 Days

```
ATTR MACRO REI2    (SECURITY sec, PERIOD TimePeriod )
        DEFINE
        COLUMN MACRO sub_values (SECURITY sec )
                VARS
                        var1
                        var2
                        num_zero
                        num_zero2
                INITIALIZE
                        var1 := High of sec - High of sec 2 units ago
                        AND
                        var2 := Low of sec - Low of sec 2 units ago
                        AND
                        num_zero := if High of sec 2 units ago < Close of sec 7 units ago AND
                                High of sec 2 units ago < Close of sec 8 units ago AND
                                High of sec < Low of sec 5 units ago   AND
                                High of sec < Low of sec 6 units ago then 0 Else 1 Endif
                        AND
                        num_zero2 := if Low of sec 2 units ago > Close of sec 7 units ago   AND
                                Low of sec 2 units ago > Close of sec 8 units ago AND
                                Low of sec > High of sec 5 units ago AND
                                Low of sec > High of sec 6 units ago then 0 Else 1 EndIf

                RETURN
                        ( num_zero * num_zero2 * var1 ) + ( var2 * num_zero * num_zero2 )

                ENDMACRO

        COLUMN MACRO AbsDailyVal ( SECURITY sec )
                VARS
                   var3
                   var4
                INITIALIZE
                   var3 := AbsVal ( High of sec - High of sec 2 units ago )
                        AND
                   var4 := AbsVal ( Low of sec - Low of sec 2 units ago )
                RETURN
                        var3 + var4

                ENDMACRO
        RETURN
            TimePeriod sum of sub_values ( sec )   / TimePeriod sum of AbsDailyVal ( sec )
        ENDMACRO
```

I recommend that you experiment with both long- and short-term versions of the indicators. By using long-term parameters, you can get a fix on the long-term trend or market environment. By using a short-term indicator to enter a trade at a low-risk entry point, you can fine-tune your entry and be confident that the trade is in the context of the market's trend.

I have included the REI and the DeMarker Indicator to illustrate how easy it is to create your own proprietary indicators. Along with a modicum of creativity, it takes a genuine desire to rise above the trading crowd. When I first attempted to accomplish such goals, there were no personal computers or software for me to rely on. This is definitely not the case today. In short, if you are determined to become successful as a trader, no such excuse exists for you not to perform such functions.

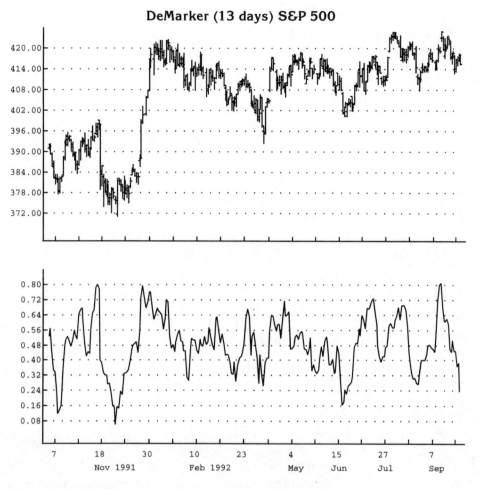

DeMarker (13 days) S&P 500

Source: Logical Information Machines, Inc. (LIM), Chicago, IL.

Figure 3.7   Note how movements above 70 and subsequently below in the DeMarker Index coincide with price peaks and, conversely, how index movement below 30 and then above 30 identifies price lows.

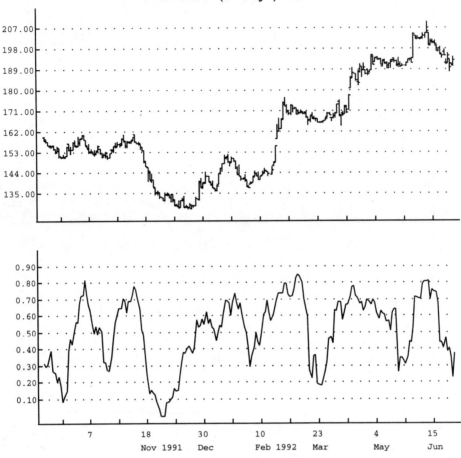

Demarker (13 days) CBS

Source: Logical Information Machines, Inc. (LIM), Chicago, IL.

Figure 3.8 Note that, once the indicator declines below 30 and above 70, potential turning points are identified.

Table 3.3   DeMarker 13 Days

```
ATTR MACRO DeMarker (SECURITY Sec, PERIOD TimePeriod )

     RETURN
        MovingAvg ( If High of Sec > High of Sec 1 unit ago
                then High of Sec - High of Sec 1 unit ago Else 0
            Endif, TimePeriod ) /
        MovingAvg ( if High of Sec > High of Sec 1 unit ago
                then High of Sec - High of Sec 1 unit ago Else 0
            Endif  + If Low of Sec > Low of Sec 1 unit ago Then 0
                else Low of Sec 1 unit ago - Low of Sec endif, TimePeriod )

     ENDMACRO
```

Chapter

Wave Analysis

Shortly after being introduced to the Elliott wave concept in the early 1970s, I sought out experts to educate me regarding this approach. Unfortunately, the only practitioners of whom I was aware were Joe Collins from St. Louis and Jack Frost from Canada. I contacted both, and they, in turn, referred me to a number of investors who had experimented with Elliott wave analysis and with Fibonacci numbers. Two individuals, both from Florida and both physicians, were recommended to me as possible resources. The experience and information they provided—more precisely, the lack thereof—were instrumental in the creation of my own approach to wave analysis.

By recounting two unrelated incidents, I might better communicate the effort in futility that I expended. I invited one doctor to Wisconsin to deliver to my business associates a speech about his interpretation of wave research. When I had arrived at the airport gate to greet him and all the passengers had deplaned and he was nowhere to be found, I called his office to determine whether he had missed the plane. His nurse/receptionist reassured me that he had made the plane; she had seen him depart. She said he would find me. I continued to wait, and eventually an individual approached and asked if I was "Tom" and I said yes. He said he recognized me because I had been walking in Fibonacci angles. I realized that I had my hands full and that my expectations were for the worst. He did not let me down—the meeting was totally unproductive and a complete disaster. Rather than give up entirely, I proceeded to interview the other wave specialist over the telephone before extending an invitation to visit. It proved to be a wise decision. My concerns were justified. I learned that the doctor was an Elliott wave and a Fibonacci enthusiast and that his life's routine had been guided by both. For example, he informed me that he had been married three times, had five children, made it a practice to work for eight consecutive days without a break, and then would take 13-day vacations. I had heard enough. I was determined to conduct my own research and draw my own conclusions regarding the subject matter. I was convinced that something of value existed but I had to uncover it myself. From the construction of the Egyptian pyramids to the conversion of kilometers to miles, the pervasiveness of Fibonacci numbers and relationships was obvious, but it was a struggle to decode and to define the role of Fibonacci and of wave behavior in the markets. My conclusions regarding Fibonacci retracements were discussed in Chapter 2. In this chapter, I discuss my wave techniques.

The elevation of wave analysis from total obscurity in the early 1970s to today's widespread acceptance is impressive to say the least. Approximately 20 years ago, I literally exhausted myself attempting to integrate the facets of both wave identification and application. Retrospectively, nothing worked better, but to apply it prospectively was next to impossible. There existed no hard and fast rules to accurately define the completion, let alone the inception of the wave pattern as it was unfolding. It was as if one were trying to catch smoke—it was visible but elusive.

Some proclaimed practitioners have applied the theory successfully, but, when asked, their explanations regarding specifics will lack consistency and will be riddled with exceptions. What has always disturbed me is, given the widespread usage of the "theory," why are the interpretations so diverse? Jokingly, I have often remarked that were one to give ten Elliott "experts" the identical chart to analyze separately, there would be ten totally different interpretations. Given all the derivation applications, such as re-tracements, if the core is lacking substance, how can its by-products be relied on? To address these seem-ingly legitimate concerns and, at the same time, capi-talize on the wave principle, I developed my own approach to wave identification. It is distinguished from the conventional version in the sense that it is definitive, concise, and logical.

Elements of the Fibonacci number series are in-terwoven throughout the Elliott wave principle. The thread stretches from the number of waves to the extent of retracements and of price projections. Un-fortunately, prior to my development of a totally me-chanical wave method, no one had produced the fabric necessary for an objective approach to wave analysis. Simply, my approach—D-Wave analysis—incorporates patterns that are defined by a series of highs and lows. The number of days selected for each series is Fibonacci-derived. Although the specific Fi-bonacci numbers used may vary, the same require-ments apply. In each instance, however, sufficient data must be accumulated to construct a workable template. Specifically, I identify a 13-day high close—a close greater than all previous 13 days' highs. Next, I locate the first close, subsequent to the 13-day high close, that is an 8-day lowest close—a close less than all previous 8 days' closes. Once those points are iden-tified, the first wave is complete. The second wave is not begun until a 21-day highest close is recorded—a close greater than all previous 21 days' closes. The second wave is considered complete once a 13-day low-est close is formed—a close less than all previous 13 days' closes. Finally, the third wave begins once a 34-day high is realized—a high greater than all previous 34 days' highs. The third wave is considered complete when a 21-day low is made—a low less than all previ-ous 21 days' lows (see Figure 4.1). As with most other illustrations presented throughout this book, the ex-amples and references demonstrating various con-cepts are replete with daily charts. This in no way implies that their application is limited to just that

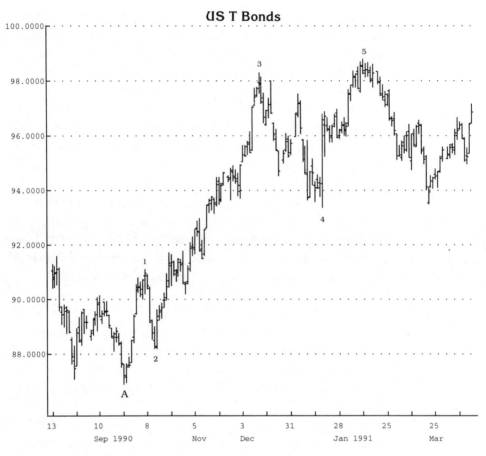

Source: Logical Information Machines, Inc. (LIM), Chicago, IL.

Figure 4.1   Identified on the chart is a map of the D-Wave concept. At point A, a 21-day low is identified—a low less than all previous 21 days' lows. Up-side movement labeled 1 actually was identified 4 days before the peak—once price closed greater than all previous 13 days' highs. D-Wave 1 was officially completed once a subsequent close was recorded that was less than all previous 8 closes. The next wave up began on the first day price closed greater than all previous 21 days' closes. This upleg was completed once price closed less than all previous 13 days' closes. The final wave up began once a 34-day high was recorded—a high greater than all previous 34 days' highs. This wave was completed once a subsequent 21-day low was made. Time is not a critical factor other than in establishing the number of days to complete waves. Price movement is important, however.

time frame. These principles apply equally to all peri-ods, whether hourly or monthly.

As is apparent by examining the sequence of numbers defining the three waves, the number of days required to establish the lows is .618 of the num-ber of days necessary to qualify the highs. A critical

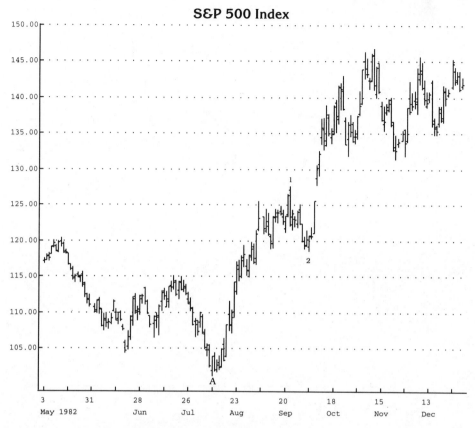

S&P 500 Index

Source: Logical Information Machines, Inc. (LIM), Chicago, IL.

Figure 4.2 Point A identifies a 21-day low close—a close less than all previous 21 days' closes—and thereby initializes D-Wave 1. Once a 13-day high close is recorded and subsequently an 8-day low close is made, D-Wave 1 is completed. Note point A, which is the 21-day low close.

consideration is the point of inception. It is essential that at least a 21-day low close be recorded before the first D-Wave count commences (see Figure 4.2). Once the D-Wave technique has been mastered, the retracement method described in Chapter 2, including the identification of the critical price and the use of the TD Retracement Qualifiers, can be applied similarly.

The Fibonacci numbers selected to identify the waves do not have to conform with those selected above. To establish a longer-term perspective, the series can begin with a greater number of days than 13. For example, 21, 34, 55, and so on, days can be used, but once the initial number is determined, all subsequent ones follow in sequence and each wave must

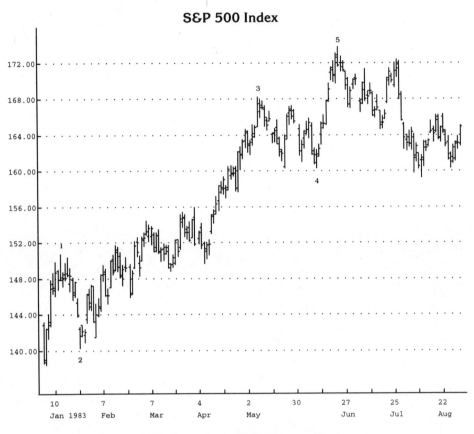

Source: Logical Information Machines, Inc. (LIM), Chicago, IL.

Figure 4.3   D-Wave 1 was properly initialized and the move to point 5 conformed well. Had this been an hourly chart instead of a daily one, the same requirements and relationships would have been adhered to.

experience a .618 number of days' low to record wave completion (see Figure 4.3).

Once the D-Wave is understood and installed, it is possible to estimate price objectives by multiplying the first wave by various Fibonacci numbers, such as 1.618, 2.618, and 3.618 (see Figures 4.4 and 4.5).

I have always believed that the holding period for trades can be categorized as short-, intermediate-, and long-term. I am certain that this terminology is acceptable to most traders. I am confident, however, that these same traders do not consider their definitions for these words to be identical to mine. Whereas they may relate these words to specific time intervals, I choose to consider them in terms of price movement.

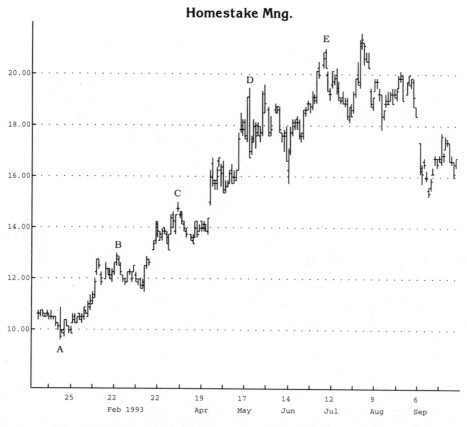

Homestake Mng.

Source: Logical Information Machines, Inc. (LIM), Chicago, IL.

Figure 4.4 By multiplying the first price leg from A-B by 1.618, 2.618, 3.618, and 4.618, the subsequent price objectives identified by points C, D, and E are projected.

In the past, volatility was not as pronounced as in recent years. Consequently, it was not unusual for a price move of 10 percent to consume a period of at least 1 to 2 months, a move of 10 to 20 percent to require 2 to 6 months, and a move of 20 to 30 percent to unfold over 6 months. As a result of large pools of funds deciding to buy or to sell at the same time because they have similar trend-following techniques or share simultaneous reception of information, prices move in vacuums quickly. What took weeks to accomplish in the past, conceivably could occur now in minutes. This is one of the major reasons why cycles are so unpredictable. In fact, this is why I feel that concentrating on time rather than price movement is

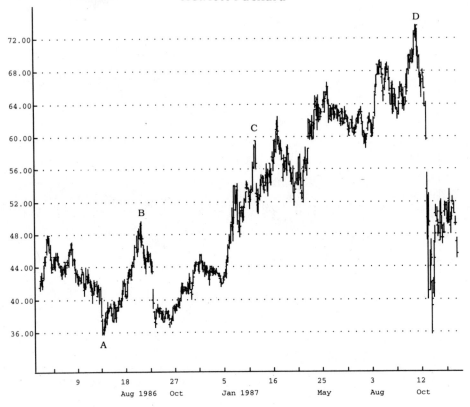

Hewlett Packard

Source: Logical Information Machines, Inc. (LIM), Chicago, IL.

Figure 4.5 Observe how, by multiplying D-Wave 1 (points A-B) by 1.618, 2.618, and 3.618, price objectives C, D, and E are identified.

outdated. D-Wave analysis acknowledges the importance of price movement, and I believe this recognition is one of the most important elements of this theory.

This has been a superficial description of D-Wave analysis, but it sends a distinct message: If the analyst subscribes to the belief that market advances and declines unfold in waves, it is not difficult to translate these movements into patterns that are objectively identifiable. Such a procedure facilitates the process of price projections and retracements. In addition, it ensures consistency and uniformity in wave identification and selection.

Chapter

5

Accumulation/ Distribution

My introduction to conventional technical analysis and to its preoccupation with subjective and artistic interpretations left me totally frustrated. Consequently, I rebelled and reverted to the other extreme: I searched for techniques that were totally objective and mechanical. At the same time I was poring over charts and divining mechanical chart techniques, I employed my economics and mathematics background to create supply–demand models capable of identifying buy and sell opportunities. My journey to accomplish this goal is described in this chapter.

Although I initially experimented and developed these various techniques for the equity markets, my research confirmed that, with a few minor adjustments, these same methods could be applied to the futures markets. Through the use of various price volume studies and formulas, I ultimately created the product that satisfied my needs.

I had learned in Economics 101 that an increase in demand occurring at the same time as static or diminishing supply translated into an advance in price. Conversely, an increase in supply that was coincident with constant or reduced demand caused price to decline.

With those principles in mind, I researched all the techniques I could find that dealt with price movement and volume. This mission included the basic on-balance volume approaches used by various market analysts. Specifically, in these instances, price activity was compared to numerous volume-weighted calculations. The basis for this type of analysis was simple: volume is considered the fuel required to move prices up and down. By successfully identifying whether the big buyers are accumulating or distributing their positions, a trader can benefit by them. Big-block stock activity is generally associated with large, sophisticated, and informed investors. To capitalize on and to participate in both their research and expectations, it is important that a market model be sensitive to shifts in supply and demand caused by their campaigns.

I have always described technicians as parasites because, in the truest sense, they are not informed nor do they care about the fundamental factors contributing to investment decisions. Their only goal is to identify and to ride the trend. An episode that occurred many years ago demonstrates the truth of this statement and best typifies the personality and attitude of a pure trader. I introduced a close friend of mine to one of the market timing systems I had developed. He was so fascinated with its ability to mechanically identify and forecast price trends that he invested his own money in a trade based on a signal generated by this system. I was unaware that he had done so. By chance, during one of our phone conversations, he was interrupted by the release of information over the newswire regarding retail sales. Apparently, the news was totally unexpected. His response was, "There goes my profit." I asked what he was talking about. He informed me that he was so fascinated by a technique that I had shared with him that he took a position in a stock that had generated a signal. He was now concerned that this fundamental news was going to affect his position adversely. I remarked that he was not a fundamentalist and he should not concern himself with the news anyway. He agreed and at the same time made the observation that whereas all the other retail stocks were reacting negatively to the news, his position was becoming more profitable. I asked the name of the stock he was involved in and he said Discount Corp. My reaction was uncontrolled laughter. This individual personified the true market analyst— he knew absolutely nothing about the fundamentals of the company in which he was invested, let alone what type of business it was in. The company he believed to be a retail operation was actually a government securities broker. This trader was a devoted disciple of the market and, with the exception of this one momentary lapse, he did not allow fundamentals to interfere with the signals generated by the systems he used. This is, admittedly, an extreme example; nevertheless, it describes the extent to which some traders ignore fundamentals and concentrate on their timing models. In their trading lives, there exists no color gray, only black and white.

Whereas fundamentals dictate the movement of prices over an extended period of time, short-run price wrinkles are best identified by employing market timing devices and techniques. Occasionally, short-term price movements successfully camouflage the underlying price trend established by the large operators, but, because volume typically precedes price movement, the prevailing trend can be identified by price change and volume analysis.

One simple technique developed to detect the basic trend merely involves the summation of daily volume; for example, if the closing price for the day is up, a positive value for that day is added to the cumulative total. Conversely, if the closing price for the day is down, a negative value for that day is added to the cumulative total. The index created is compared to the actual daily price movement, and divergences are identified to forecast price flow (see Figure 5.1).

Another, more complicated method analyzes each transaction (tick) and continuously recalculates the index by multiplying the price change by the number of shares (contracts). Rather than scrutinizing each trade, however, other technicians isolate only the large-block (more than 10,000-share) transactions, assuming they are initiated by informed, sophisticated investors whose degree of aggressiveness

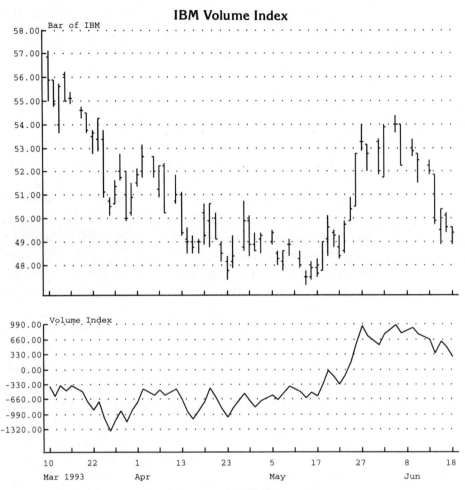

Figure 5.1 The concept behind this method is simple—volume precedes price movement. If the price close is up versus the previous day, accumulation is taking place. If the price close is down versus the previous day, distribution is dominant for that day. Practitioners of this method believe that, camouflaged behind seemingly random price movements, a cumulative index of accumulation and distribution will alert traders to the true market picture.

is revealed by their price concessions. Other volume analysts rely on price change and volume, but merely compute their calculations daily at the conclusion of trading. They multiply the price change by the volume on that particular day to create an index (see Figure 5.2).

All these techniques were helpful, but none fulfilled my needs. I wanted something more exact and

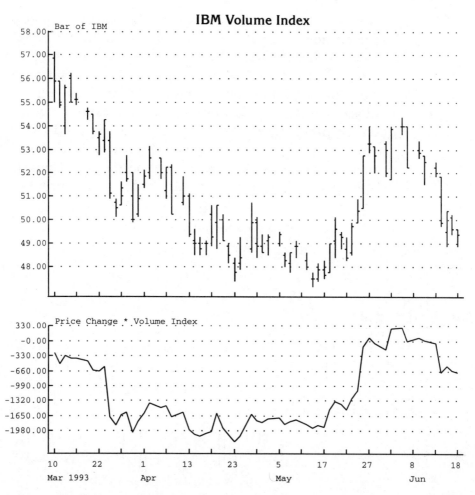

Source: Logical Information Machines, Inc. (LIM), Chicago, IL.

Figure 5.2 By accounting for not only volume but also for the extent of the price movement (price concessions) from one close to the next, an index of accumulation–distribution can be enhanced.

sensitive. A close friend and fellow market timer, Larry Williams, was working on precisely the same project. He convinced me that the proper reference point was the current day's open, rather than the previous day's closing price. Although all price services—whether presented daily in the newspaper or in other media sources, or obtained from quote machines—report price change from the previous day's close, this practice does not represent a true picture of price accumulation or distribution. It is not difficult to conclude that what occurred yesterday is history. Because of news events, the open could spike up or down and, consequently, a particular day's close could be higher than yesterday's close. As a result, what ostensibly appears to be accumulation or distribution based on the relationship of the current close versus the previous day's close would in actuality be precisely the opposite when compared to the same day's opening price (see Figure 5.3). Furthermore, to account for those exceptional cases when the open price is significantly different from the previous

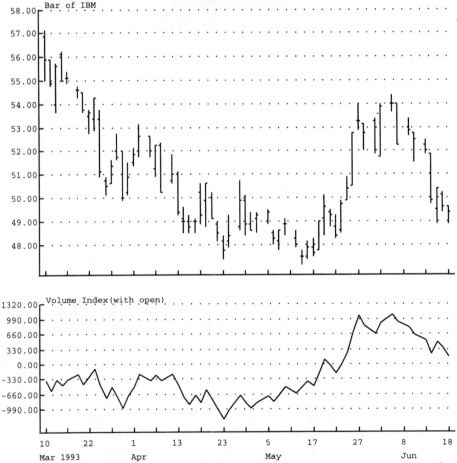

Source: Logical Information Machines, Inc. (LIM), Chicago, IL.

Figure 5.3 What occurred yesterday is history. A more meaningful relationship than closing price movement is the relationship between a price close and that same day's opening price. If the close is greater than the open, accumulation has taken place; conversely, if the close is less than the open, distribution has taken place.

day's close, an adjustment formula can be inserted to account for the price gap and to deemphasize the movement from the current day's open and close.

It was apparent that the current day's price range was a major component in measuring accumulation and distribution. By comparing the movement from the current day's close and open with that of the high to the low and by incorporating the factor of volume, a significant basis for a legitimate supply–demand model can be constructed. What I finally arrived at, however, was something considerably more complex and sensitive to shifts in supply and demand than this relatively crude approach. Specifically, although the relationship between price activity and the index was a good indicator of the direction of price, it was virtually impossible to compare the relative attractiveness of various securities because some issues were much more active (in volume) than others. Let me describe and explain in more detail how I was able to reconcile the issues of both comparing and ranking securities.

Just because I present my conclusions regarding the relationship between price change and volume, I do not mean to imply that my approach is necessarily the best; rather, it is the one I created and rely on after having researched and examined countless others. Its features are its logic, simplicity, and versatility, as well as its integration of numerous analytical approaches. Once mastered, it is designed to afford the user the ability to evaluate on a relative basis a large number of securities. Ideally, he will be able also to draw inferences regarding the cause of price advances or declines—was the rally the beginning of a sustained advance or just short covering? Rather than recite numerous other benefits derived from the techniques described herein, I will present them and highlight their advantages and disadvantages.

The techniques that follow are related, and the composite approach presented evolved over a period of many years. The creation of the nucleus was the most critical element in the process. Often, I challenged the logic and the foundation of my basic assumptions. Given what was available in the public domain, however, I was convinced that the basis was sufficiently sound to support all my derivative studies. As I discussed above, the critical item in distinguishing between accumulation (demand) and distribution (supply) is the reference point selected. Many years after I had concluded that the open was the proper pivot price for almost all measures of accumulation/distribution, I had this supposition confirmed by one of the major operators in the stock market. More specifically, everyone is aware of the stature and dominance assigned the specialists on the New York Stock Exchange. I had the pleasure of establishing a special kinship with one of the most respected of these individuals. I shared with him my theories and formulas regarding accumulation and distribution and the importance of the open price. He was amazed to learn of both my discoveries and my approach to analysis. He indicated to me that I had accomplished mathematically precisely what he had acquired intuitively over many years on the floor. To translate it into a workable code enabling an investor to monitor a large number of securities simultaneously was an effort he had previously believed unattainable. His endorsement reinforced my commitment to this method and further research.

Although the formulas are elementary, in order to fully appreciate their power and potential I recommend you experiment thoroughly with every facet of the concepts of accumulation/distribution presented (see Figure 5.4). The basis of all measures includes this formula:

$$\frac{\text{Close–open}}{\text{High–low}} \times \begin{array}{l}\text{Volume for that}\\\text{particular day}\end{array}$$

In other words, this calculation depicts the relationship of the close on a particular day to that day's open. If it is positive, it can be argued that price accumulation has taken place; if it is negative, price distribution has occurred. The intensity of the accumulation or distribution can be determined by relating movement from the open to the close, comparing it with the

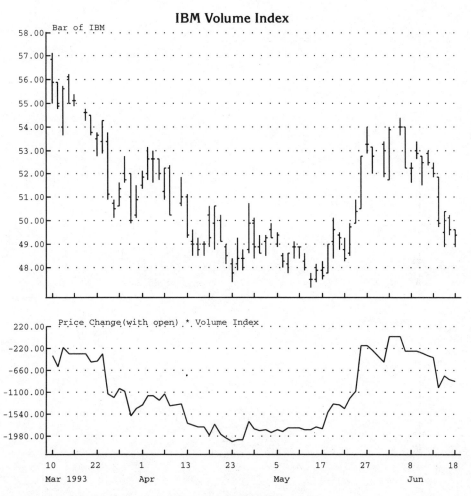

Source: Logical Information Machines, Inc. (LIM), Chicago, IL.

Figure 5.4 By using the price change from close to open, as well as the volume, another index can be constructed.

price range for that day (high to low), and then multiplying this ratio by that day's volume. In and of itself, this index value, when run cumulatively and compared with the underlying price activity, is a good indicator of future price movement.

Before discussing the technique for standardizing securities, it is important to present an adjustment to this formula to compensate for significant opening price gaps of eight percent or more (see Figure 5.5). In these rare instances, even if price retraces back to the open, the exceptional inflation or deflation in the open

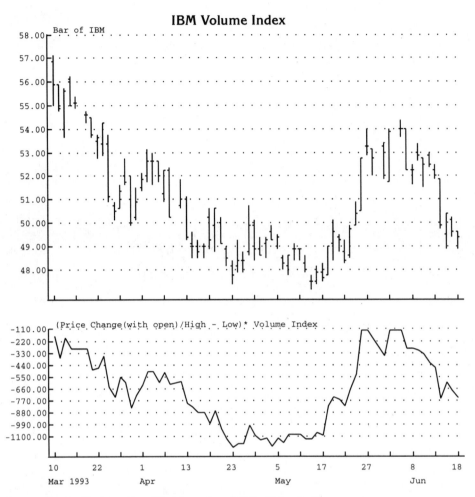

Source: Logical Information Machines, Inc. (LIM), Chicago, IL.

Figure 5.5(a) By dividing the price movement from close to open by the price movement traversed for the entire day, the degree of aggressiveness is determined. For example, if price were to open on its low and close on its high on a particular day, it would suggest a more intensive buying campaign than if price were to open or close at the daily price midrange.

price must be considered by introducing a formula that supersedes the original one. To calculate the buying (accumulation) pressure with an open or close of eight percent or greater than the previous day's close, the difference between today's high and yesterday's close is added to the difference between today's close and today's low. From this sum, the difference between today's high and today's close is subtracted. In turn, this value is divided by the difference between today's high and yesterday's close. The volume for the day is

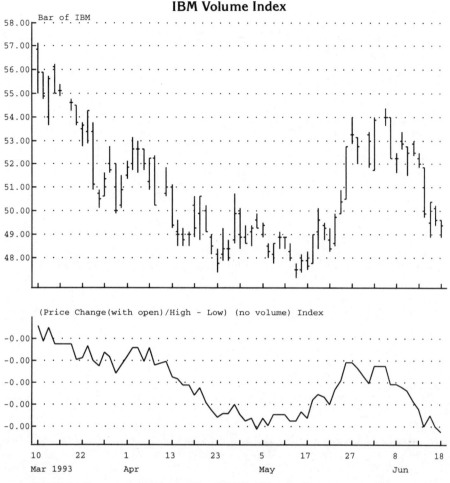

Source: Logical Information Machines, Inc. (LIM), Chicago, IL.

Figure 5.5(b)   One chart [5-5(a)] illustrates with volume included and the other [5-5(b)] with no volume.

then multiplied by this value and added to the cumulative index. Conversely, in order to calculate the selling (distribution) pressure with an open eight percent or more *less than* the previous day's close, the difference between yesterday's close and today's low is added to the difference between today's high and today's close. From this sum, the difference between today's close and today's low is subtracted. In turn, this value is divided by the difference between yesterday's close and today's low. The volume for the day is then multiplied by this value and added to the cumulative index (see Figure 5.6).

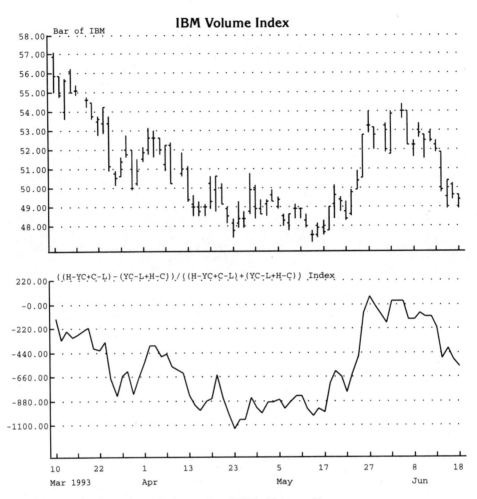

Source: Logical Information Machines, Inc. (LIM), Chicago, IL.

Figure 5.6 When an open occurs that is eight percent or more greater than or less than the previous day's close, an adjustment must be made to accentuate this atypical price behavior. Additionally, this formula can be used in lieu of opening prices when they are unavailable.

Should the open price be unobtainable for any reason, a version of the gap compensation formula would serve as a credible substitute. A few revisions are required, however:

1. Calculate the difference between today's high and yesterday's close (if less than zero, then ignore) and the difference between today's close and today's low, to arrive at a measure of the buying pressure (buying pressure).

2. Determine the difference between yesterday's close and today's low (if less than zero, then ignore), and add the difference between today's high and today's close (selling pressure).

3. Add together the buying and selling pressure, and divide this value into the buying pressure figure if today is an up close; divide this value into the selling pressure if today is a down close.

4. Multiply this number by the total volume for the day and add to the cumulative index (see Figure 5.7a).

What you have learned so far are variations of what you may have already seen in the public domain. What I am about to share with you now is proprietary and essential to the task of comparing various securities to determine relative attractiveness. The concept is easy and straightforward, but it is important that you follow each step to ensure complete understanding and total mastery.

After the formula for calculating accumulation/distribution has been selected—I recommend the one using the open reference with the adjustment for open gaps of eight percent or more—a schedule of various time intervals is to be selected. I recommend an array of Fibonacci numbers beginning with five days and extending to 13, 21, 34, 55, 89, 144, 233, and 377 days. Each day, a value representing buying or selling pressure appears. Add together all the positive (buying pressure) numbers over the prescribed period of days, and then add together all the negative (selling pressure) numbers over that same period. Then divide the sum of all the buying pressure values by the absolute value of the sum of all the buying pressure values plus all the selling pressure values. This number is a ratio defining the buying pressure divided by the total activity (buying pressure plus selling pressure) and can be converted to a percentage by merely multiplying times 100 percent.

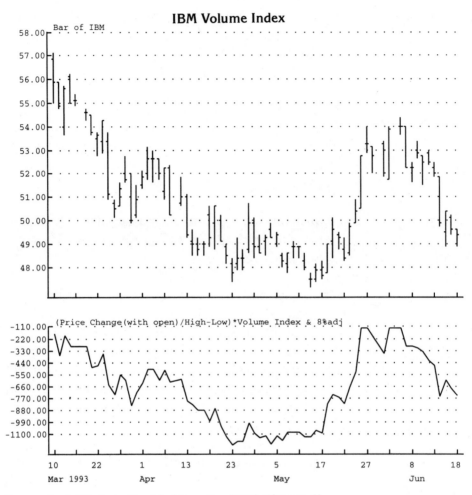

Source: Logical Information Machines, Inc. (LIM), Chicago, IL.

Figure 5.7(a)   The adjustment for exceptional (eight percent or more) open gaps is introduced into the basic formula. Figure 5.7(a) includes volume.

In order to get the flavor of what is taking place within the dynamics of the market, this procedure can be applied to other time periods in the same manner. These percentages measure the demand over various time intervals, so it is possible to relate one security to another to determine which is being more aggressively accumulated or distributed. A chart of each security is even more helpful in displaying the movement of this oscillator (see Figure 5.8).

Even more important, however, is an indicator that displays the rate of change of the percentages. In fact, my experience has proven this value to be the

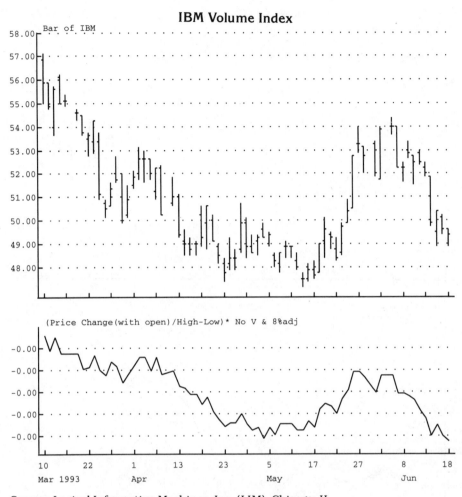

Source: Logical Information Machines, Inc. (LIM), Chicago, IL.

Figure 5.7(b)   This chart does not include volume.

most reliable in identifying attractive investment opportunities. The rate of change is calculated easily:
divide the current day's percentage by the percentage
X days ago. I typically work with Fibonacci numbers.
Once a particular number is selected, I calculate the
rate of change by dividing the value that day by the
value at least four Fibonacci levels lower. For example,
if I employ an 89-day series, to calculate the rate of
change I would compare today's value with that of 13
days ago—in the Fibonacci series, 13 increases next to
21, 34, 55, then 89. As you can see, 13 is positioned
four degrees beneath 89. If one were to use a 144-day
series, then a comparison between the current day's

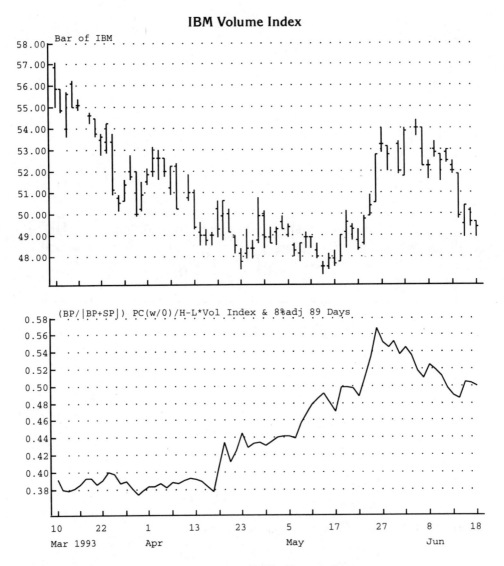

Source: Logical Information Machines, Inc. (LIM), Chicago, IL.

Figure 5.8   It has always been difficult to relate the attractiveness of one security versus another. By calculating the percentage of buying pressure divided by the total pressure (both buying and selling), comparisons can be
made. This measure is a serious breakthrough in trading analytics.

value and that 21 days ago would be used; if one were
to use a 233-day series, then a comparison between
that day's value and the value 34 days earlier would be
selected. Keep in mind that these are merely suggestions. You may have greater success at using other
number series or comparing other periods of rates
of change. Once selected, however, the period should

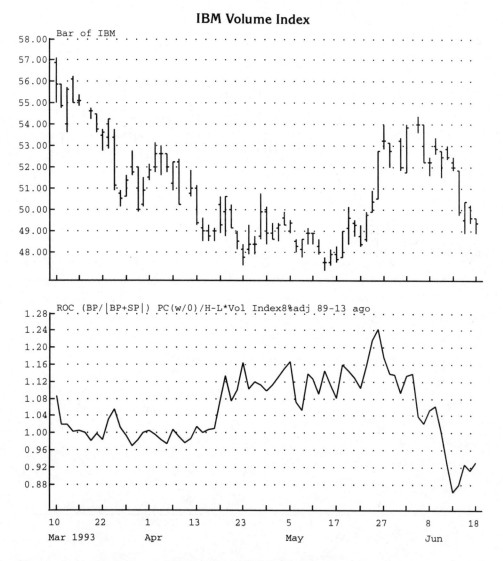

Source: Logical Information Machines, Inc. (LIM), Chicago, IL.

Figure 5.9 By determining the rate of change of buying pressure divided by the total pressure (both buying and selling), the degree of aggressiveness among various securities, as well as for individual securities, can be measured.

remain static for all securities compared. For example, if an 89-day value is used for one stock and the rate of change is based on the value 13 days prior, then the same time periods should be used when evaluating the relative appeal of other stock candidates (see Figure 5.9). Once a value is selected, the index for most stocks will move within the same band. Experimentation with that index will yield the parameters associated with

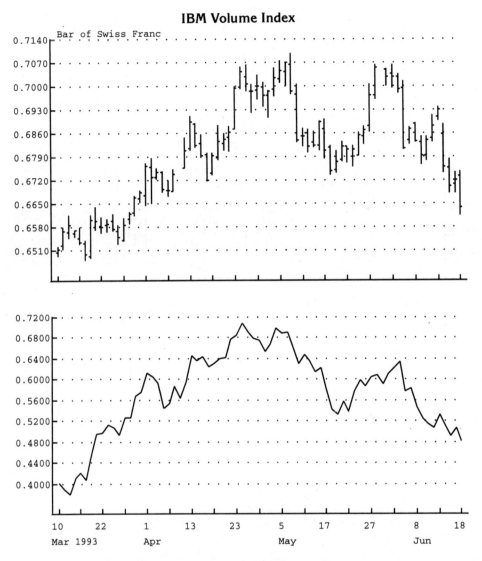

IBM Volume Index

Bar of Swiss Franc

Source: Logical Information Machines, Inc. (LIM), Chicago, IL.

Figure 5.10   No volume and a different time period (34 days versus 34 days 5 days ago) are presented on this chart.

price tops and bottoms. Generally, the rate of change of this index will reverse prior to the actual price turns. Together with other techniques, entry and exit prices can be identified and the relative attraction of a situation can be compared with other opportunities.

The above technique describes an accumulation/ distribution model for stocks. The same approach can be applied to futures, with one exception. Whereas stocks have no restrictions as to the upside or downside movement they can traverse daily, futures have prescribed daily price limits because of the extreme leverage involved in those markets. When price moves limit, trading is virtually suspended. Although transactions can be effected at those price extremes, depending on the pool size looking to buy or sell, the volume the market is capable of producing may be significantly less than if there were no price limits. To account for this pent-up supply or demand, I recommend combining all consecutive days extending from the first day a limit move occurs until the last day of the series. The open price of the first day and the closing price of the last day, as well as the range and the volume for the entire period, are treated as if they were one day. This method incorporates the basic approach described and compensates for the shortcoming associated with limit moves. Some success is derived by excluding volume totally and running the formula described in Figure 5.9 with various other time periods both long and short term (see Figure 5.10).

As you can see, the model just described has application to both equities and futures. Variations of this model have equal application to these same markets with similar results. As with every other technique presented in this book, the best results are realized in combination with other proven approaches, thus enhancing the prospects of trading success. Consequently, my recommendation is not only to experiment and to introduce the accumulation/distribution model into your trading tool kit but also to utilize other methods that confirm your trading rules.

Chapter

6

Moving Averages

For many years now, one of the most popular trend-following methods has been the moving average. The simplicity of its construction and the ease of its interpretation contribute to its widespread usage and acceptance. Unfortunately, this tool's success is derived from a particular market's ability to trend. My research indicates that markets generally move in trading ranges and trend much less frequently. Historical observations suggest that, approximately 75 to 80 percent of the time, price of a particular security tends to move in a trading range. On the other hand, 20 to 25 percent of the time, price trends are either up or down. Furthermore, additional research shows that price accelerates in a downtrend generally about two to two and a half times faster than price in an uptrend. This phenomenon can be easily accounted for by the fact that whereas investors typically accumulate a position over a period of time, their recognition of a price decline is immediate and their tendency is to liquidate the entire position at one time.

The most common and basic calculation of the moving average is arithmatic and involves only adding together the closing prices of a security over a prescribed period of time, dividing this sum by the total number of entries, and then plotting that period's value on a chart coincident with that interval's price range. Unfortunately, this is the common practice but it is not necessarily the ideal or the correct one. Most market timers ignore or fail to recognize many questions that arise. Specifically:

- Why is each time period equally weighted when in fact the most recent price activity is more important?

- Why is the final calculation plotted on a chart immediately beneath the last price entry when an average is calculated?

- Why are only the closing prices averaged and other critical price points such as open, high, and low overlooked?

- Why are some periods of time more popular than others?

- Why are moving averages so widely accepted and used when in most instances they are applied to trading range markets, which causes the user to get continuously whipsawed?

My experience suggests that the results achieved by using traditional moving averages are no better than those realized by using most other conventional trend-following approaches. Moving averages are easily calculated and understood and can be found on most quote service graphics displays and in almost all graphics software packages. Don't confuse this universal availability with utility and trading success, however. I have found that, in this industry, there is no correlation between acceptance/usage and performance results—in fact, precisely the opposite is true in most instances.

Given some exceptions, despite extensive research, I have uncovered only a few circumstances in which moving averages can be applied and respectable results can be expected. Specifically, by definition, moving averages identify turning points in trend well after they have occurred. As I stated earlier, markets operate within a trading range most of the time. Occasionally, however, prices do break out of this pattern. My adaptations to moving average analysis have proven to be worthwhile in those breakouts because the risk of being whipsawed is diminished considerably.

Basically, the various moving average techniques I recommend all cope differently with the issue of trading range whipsaws. One version projects moving averages into the future; another averages highs, lows, and closes for a period of time to create a fictitious average price to compare with the moving average; and still another employs a moving average only when price breaks out of a trading range. A description of each is presented here.

Conventional trading analysis provides for the moving average entries to be aligned with the trading days such that the last moving average entry coincides with the last price entry. There is nothing sacred about this particular relationship, and this practice has always bothered me. I experimented with centering the moving average and realized some improvement in performance results. Instead of calculating the moving average and positioning the values beneath the most recent entry, as most traders would, I experimented with the technique of having the projected average coincide with the current day's price. In a sense, you might say that 38 percent of the moving average band appears prior to the current price entry, and 62 percent is projected into the future. In other words, 62 percent of the moving average has been projected into the future. I found that this shift retained the pattern of the moving average and at the same time reduced the likelihood of whipsaws inherent in trading ranges.

Another approach for calculating a series of moving averages attempts to avoid the problem of trading ranges and of whipsaws by making certain that the short-term moving average exceeds upside the long-term moving average in the case of a buy signal, and that the short-term moving average exceeds downside the long-term moving average in the case of a sell signal. At the same time, both moving averages must exceed either a fictitious price peak or price trough that is an average of the most recent two days' highs and two days' lows. I have been the most comfortable using moving averages of 5 and 21 days' duration. To demonstrate just how this method works, calculate the value of each moving average by summing the opens, highs, lows, and closes over each respective time period. Next, project both averages into the future: in the case of the 5-day average, project 3 days into the future; in the case of the 21-day moving average, project 13 days into the future. If the 5-day projected value is more than the 21-day projected value, then look to buy; if the 5-day projected value is less than the 21-day projected value, look to sell.

Performance results can be enhanced further by making certain that both averages exceed the hypothetical two-day price high (buy) or low (sell). Further improvements are realized if both moving averages are declining or advancing together. Finally, by making certain that the 5-day average is greater than the 21-day average for a buy signal and less than the 21-day average for a sell signal, you should realize improved results.

To avoid a multitude of signals while locked in a trading range market, I created a moving average system that only became active when price recorded either a 13-day-high low or a 13-day-low high. Let me explain this concept further. If price advances and it records a low greater than all previous 12 lows, then a 3-day moving average of lows is installed and followed for a period of 4 trading days to identify a place to sell. Conversely, if price declines and it records a high less than all previous 12 highs, then a 3-day moving average of highs is installed and followed for a period of 4 trading days to identify a place to buy. The moving average is active for a period of only 4 days after the higher low or the lower high is recorded. As you can see, the application of the moving averages is dependent on the fulfillment of various prerequisites. Other variations of this approach can also be applied. In every instance, however, the key ingredient of any approach is its ability to remain dormant while price moves sideways. Once price breaks out of the trading range, the technique should be sufficiently sensitive to detect any movement that would precede a trend reversal.

For many years, I observed a central tendency for price activity to move within a band defined by a moving average that was identified by multiplying each day's price low by 110 percent and each day's price high by 90 percent. This band can be smoothed by multiplying an average of the previous 3 days' lows and highs and by increasing the band factors to 115 percent and 85 percent. When price exceeded this moving average band, overbought and oversold readings were generated. The percentages presented can be adapted to specific markets.

One technique I developed many years ago I call the TD Moving Average technique. It is designed to initiate buy and sell signals on the first day both of two moving averages—a long term and a short term—turn up or down simultaneously for the first time. Generally, the short-term average responds first and subsequently the long term confirms—that is the day action is to be taken. In other words, the first instance they both move up or down versus the previous day's TD Moving Average readings is the trigger day. Typically, the two moving average periods I use are 13 and 55 days, but the latter period has been adjusted to as many as 65 days.

I believe another approach has merit but, because of both software and data constraints, I have been unable to test it. This method involves identifying and averaging the median (middle) price recorded each day for a particular period of the day. I plan to experiment with variations of this technique now that I possess the software required; I am awaiting the necessary data.

My moving average techniques are unconventional. They have been designed to counteract the nemesis of all moving average approaches—trading range and sideways markets. I believe that these methods circumvent the obstacles confronting the average trader. Together with the other trading ideas presented throughout the book, these approaches can be implemented to give the savvy trader a market edge.

Chapter

7

Sequential™

At the time I entered the investment business, it was commonplace to attempt to identify price tops and bottoms by using cycles. The length of these cycles was determined by calculating either the number of days from one price low to a succeeding price low or the number of days from a particular price low to a subsequent price peak (see Figures 7.1 and 7.2). This method of market timing is subjective and, because the periods are not static, it does not lend itself to statistical analysis and testing. In fact, the interpretation of cycles is sufficiently vague that, often, where a low or a high might be expected to be found, a condition called "inversion" occurs instead: prices actually do the opposite of that which was anticipated. I was disturbed by this lack of predictability. Consequently, I experimented with the application of the Fibonacci time series to cycles and obtained somewhat better results but nothing extraordinary.

I have always been skeptical of the practice of relying on cycles to identify price tops and bottoms. It is difficult for me to accept the fact that an arbitrarily derived number of days possesses repetitive properties. Quite to the contrary, my research studies suggest that the price action of some trading days is actually meaningless.

Consequently, I researched exhaustively to create a technique that would employ a mechanized timing device to identify price highs

US Bond (weekly)

Source: Logical Information Machines, Inc. (LIM), Chicago, IL.

Figure 7.1   The approximate period of time from a price low to a subsequent price low is 39 weeks. Each low for this cycle is marked with an X.

and lows as they occurred. I experimented endlessly to determine what price relationships typically appeared prior to and coincident with market turning points. Let me describe, in basic terms and by using simple examples, the process I followed.

Once demand exceeds supply, price advances. Whether this advance is due to short covering, purchase recommendations, positive news, or any other factors is immaterial. At a certain point in time, figuratively speaking, all the potential buyers will have bought. Unless there is a catalyst to entice a new crop of buyers, the market is vulnerable to decline for two reasons: (1) an exhaustion of buying or (2) an increase in the pace of selling. My experience confirms that,

Gold weekly

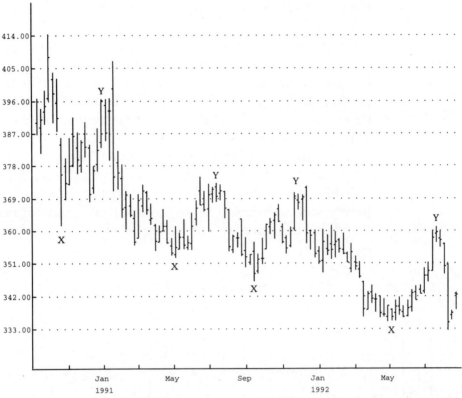

Source: Logical Information Machines, Inc. (LIM), Chicago, IL.

Figure 7.2   The approximate number of weeks from a price low to a subsequent high close is 10 weeks. The periods are marked X and Y.

typically, prices peak not because of sophisticated and knowledgeable sellers' accurate identification of the price high, but rather because the "last buyer" has bought. Conversely, as supply exceeds demand, price declines. Whether this selloff is attributable to bad news, sell recommendations, short selling, or any other factor is immaterial. Eventually, however, all the potential sellers will have sold. My research has proven that price bottoms are made once the last seller has sold and, by default, price moves up. In fact, when aggressive buying prematurely occurs at an interim low, typically it is associated with a short covering rally. Consequently, after the buying frenzy diminishes, a price vacuum is created and ultimately price declines even faster and further until a new equilibrium level between supply and demand is established (see Figure 7.3). At that point, if the dynamics are right and the selling pressure has been exhausted, price has an opportunity to reverse upside.

As price advances, it approaches its ultimate peak; conversely, as price declines, it moves closer to its eventual low. These comments are made not to insult your intelligence, but rather to emphasize the obvious: selling into strength and buying into weakness are practices often overlooked and believed unattainable by traders. As a result, most traders are trend followers who subscribe to the notion that a particular trend will continue in force. They believe that attempts

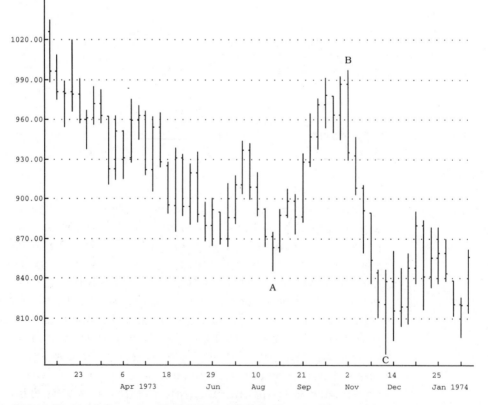

DJIA (weekly)

Source: Logical Information Machines, Inc. (LIM), Chicago, IL.

Figure 7.3 Observe the 10-week advance (A-B) and the abrupt, severe 5-week decline to new lows (C).

to buy into a declining market are akin to catching falling daggers. To overcome this fear, some traders utilize cycles, but as I mentioned earlier, cycles are too arbitrary and subjective. Consequently, I created a technique that incorporates in vague terms the concept of cycles without the handicap of time rigidity.

Whereas cycles traders employ a prescribed time series, I rely on a dynamic set of variables that adjusts to market action. In other words, I wait for the market to speak to me as the price movement unfolds. Actions speak louder than words, and what better source of market direction is there than the market itself? All information known, including all the hopes and fears of traders, is translated into one important item—price. Should unexpected developments regarding market fundamentals arise and the supply–demand equation be shifted as a result, the price movement should reflect this change. Just as the market's price personality constantly undergoes change, so too any system that attempts to identify price tops and bottoms must adapt to these character swings in money flow and measure them precisely. This major deficiency of conventional cycles analysis makes it inferior to the versatile approach I will share with you.

My research confirms the fact that, prior to a price top or bottom, the market announces its intentions regarding price direction loud and clear to any trader willing to listen. Specifically, the market forewarns the trader whether it is predisposed toward a price top or toward a price bottom. In other words, the market's environment or inclination to top or to bottom is first defined by this setup phase. Because this entire approach is mechanical, as are the additional filters required to actually generate the buy and sell signals, I developed a checklist to simplify this process (see below). The feature of this approach is its design to buy into weakness and to sell into strength. Once all the prerequisites are satisfied in the order required, a signal occurs. Hence, the name Sequential™ was given to the system.

The procedure followed to establish a Sequential buy or sell signal is straightforward and uncomplicated.

In fact, the simplicity associated with its implementation concerned me at the time I developed the technique. I was puzzled that no one else had previously discovered and integrated the same time series and price relationships. Continuously, I checked and rechecked my studies to make certain that I had not overlooked some key element. Keep in mind that the period of development and testing was not by any means recent—this all took place in the 1970s. It was conceived and researched prior to the era of computers. Since that time, this technique has had universal application to various markets, including stocks, futures, and indexes. As a result of additional research, I have developed enhancements to the original Sequential™, but the core of the method still exists and thrives. How many other definitive market timing approaches designed to anticipate price tops and bottoms have endured and have withstood a similar test of time? Not many, if any at all.

Setup

To generate a sequential buy signal, the market environment must first be predisposed to rally. My research determined that a prerequisite to a buy is a particular relationship among closing prices over a period of nine consecutive days. Specifically, once a period of at least nine consecutive trading closes less than the close four trading days earlier is recorded, then the buy setup is complete. For example, if the close of trading on Friday is less than the close of trading on that same week's Monday (assuming trading occurred on Thursday, Wednesday, and Tuesday), one day of a possible set of nine is defined. Had the close of Friday been equal to or greater than the close on Monday, however, this day would not have qualified as one day of a nine-day buy setup.

Figures 7.4 and 7.5 describe the requirements for a valid buy setup. The first day of the nine-day buy setup must be preceded by a close on the trading day

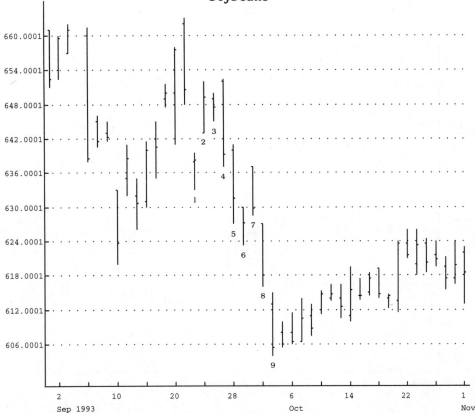

Source: Logical Information Machines, Inc. (LIM), Chicago, IL.

Figure 7.4   Requirements for a valid buy setup.

immediately before it that is greater than or equal to the close four trading days earlier (see Figure 7.6). As is apparent from these examples, it is not uncommon to witness a short-term bottom or even a price reversal upon completion of the nine-day setup. Unless the market is in a free fall or in a short-term correction within an uptrend, this short-term price hiccup is just a reprieve in the downtrend and the decline should resume.

In order to generate a sequential sell signal, the market environment must be predisposed to a decline. The prerequisite for a sell setup is exactly the opposite of the prerequisite for a buy signal. A buy setup requires a series of nine consecutive days' closes less than the close four trading days earlier; a sell setup

Copper

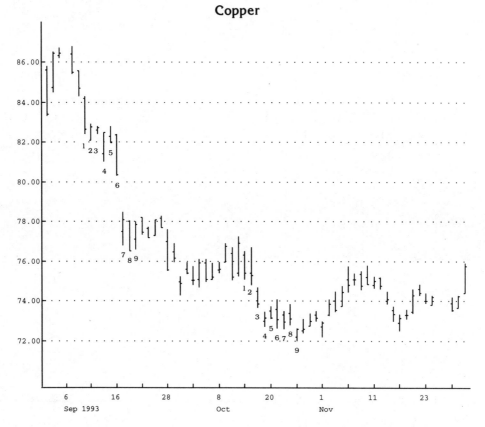

Source: Logical Information Machines, Inc. (LIM), Chicago, IL.

Figure 7.5 The first close less than the close four trading days prior to it is marked with an X. All subsequent days are marked numerically. *It is not uncommon for price to reverse or move sideways once the setup of nine days is recorded.*

requires a series of nine consecutive trading days' closes greater than the close four trading days earlier. For example, if the close of trading on Friday is greater than the close of trading on that same week's Monday (assuming trading occurred on Thursday, Wednesday, and Tuesday), one day of a possible set of nine has been defined. Had the close on Friday been less than or equal to the close of Monday, this day would not have qualified as one day of a nine-day sell setup. The requirements for a valid sell setup are described in Figures 7.7 and 7.8. The first day of the nine-day sell setup must be preceded by a close on the trading day immediately before it that is less than the close four

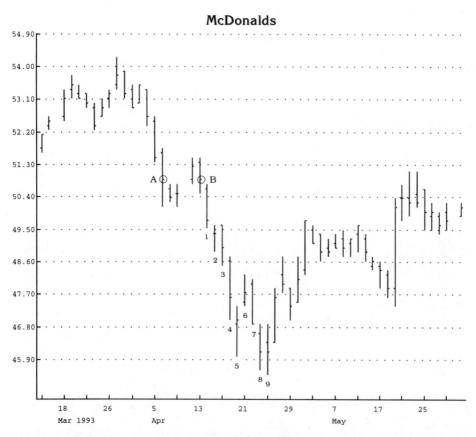

Source: Logical Information Machines, Inc. (LIM), Chicago, IL.

Figure 7.6 The close on day B is greater than or equal to the close on day A. The next day's close is less than the close four days earlier and is counted as day one of the setup. Note how price bottomed out on the ninth day of the setup.

trading days earlier (see Figure 7.9). Similar to the buy setup, a derivative benefit of the nine-day sell setup is the identification of a short-term high once the setup is formed. Unless the market is in a blow-off phase or the overall trend is defined as down, this pullback should be temporary, however, and the advance should resume.

As you can see, the setup is very simple to establish. Either it requires nine consecutive trading days' closes less than the trading days' close four days before each for a buy signal, or it requires nine consecutive trading days' closes greater than the trading days' close four days before each for a sell signal. It is important that:

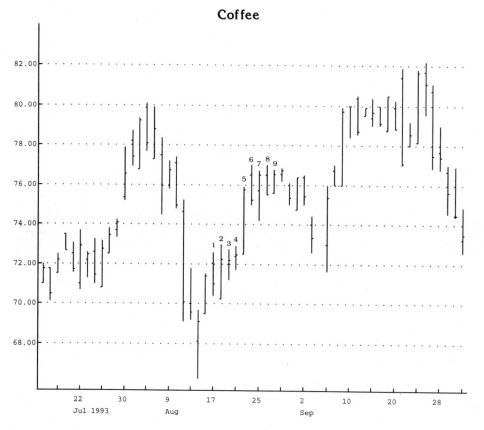

Coffee

Source: Logical Information Machines, Inc. (LIM), Chicago, IL.

Figure 7.7 Nine consecutive days in which the close is greater than the close four trading days earlier are counted on this chart—in other words, a sell setup has been completed. Notice the price "hiccup" or "stutter" as I describe it upon completion of this series—although it is not always the case, frequently the price movement stalls or reverses upon setup completion.

1. Each of the three days between the current trading day and the trading day's close four days ago is a trading day;

2. The trading day's close of the day prior to day one of a buy setup is greater than the close of the trading day four days earlier, and the trading day's close of the day prior to day one of a sell setup is less than the close of the trading four days earlier;

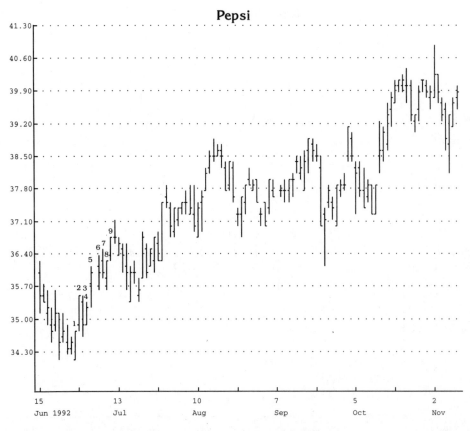

Source: Logical Information Machines, Inc. (LIM), Chicago, IL.

Figure 7.8   A series of nine consecutive closes greater than the close four trading days earlier defines the sell setup. Note that price established short-term peaks upon completion of the setup period—the ninth day.

3. If the close of a trading day is equal to the close of the trading day four days before it, the setup series is interrupted and must begin anew;

4. The series of consecutive closes may exceed nine but the required period for a valid setup is satisfied once the requirement of nine consecutive closes is met.

There is a natural rhythm defined by the setup series of nine consecutive closes greater than or less than the

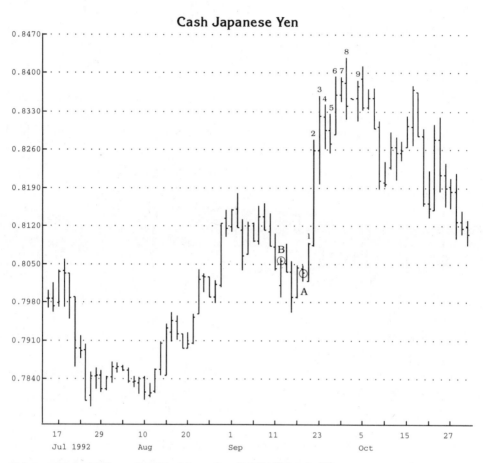

Cash Japanese Yen

Source: Logical Information Machines, Inc. (LIM), Chicago, IL.

Figure 7.9 On the day prior to the first day of the sell setup, the close (A) was less than the close four days earlier (B).

close four days earlier. Generally, the market will experience a reversal or a stabilization in price at that time. In fact, as mentioned earlier, in some instances, price will record a significant turn at just that point. These observations are universal and apply to all markets and to all time intervals.

I made an observation several years ago regarding the comparison between the most recent price setup and the most recent price setup in the other price direction. As the current price setup is being formed, I compare (1) the extreme price peak or low—depending on whether the movement is up or down—recorded from the first day of the most recent setup

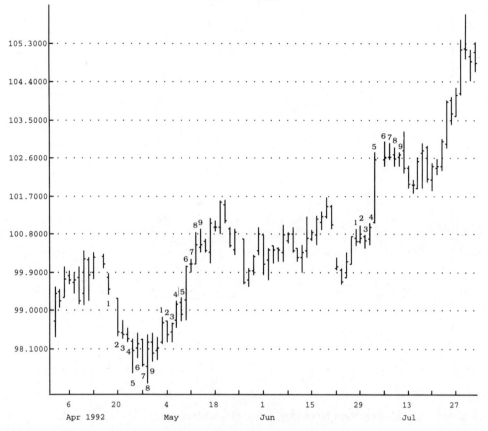

US T Bonds

Source: Logical Information Machines, Inc. (LIM), Chicago, IL.

Figure 7.10 Note how the nine consecutive up closes (setup) in early–mid May exceeded the nine consecutive down closes (setup) recorded in late April.

through its completion with (2) that of the most recent "inactive" setup through its completion. An inactive setup is defined as one in which the series of consecutive closes versus closes four days earlier has numbered at least nine but has been interrupted and one in which the trend contradicts the current setup (see Figures 7.10 and 7.11). By definition, this must be the case because the current setup occurs in the other direction. Although, technically speaking, the setup is comprised of a series of nine consecutive closes greater than the close four trading days earlier for a sell (and less than for a buy), the comparison of the two setups does not necessarily require the

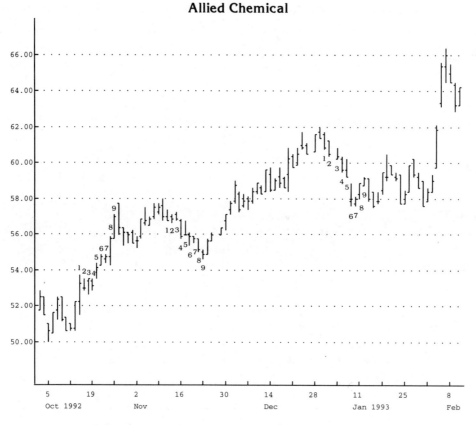

Source: Logical Information Machines, Inc. (LIM), Chicago, IL.

Figure 7.11   In both instances (Figure 7.10 as well), you can see a series of setups. In both cases, note short-term top (bottom) generally seen after nine setup—price "hiccup" or "stutter" if you will.

completion of the entire current series of closes because the peak or trough can exceed the trough or the peak—depending on whether the current setup is up or down—of the inactive setup before the setup is completed. In fact, it may not be formed at all. This particular technique has enabled me to define the trend of various markets on numerous occasions, and it is a valuable derivative benefit of a Sequential™ setup.

A vital element is required to validate the Sequential setup. Its absence underscores the fact that the market is in a runaway phase. For example, if price is declining in a waterfall manner, it is important that a retardation of the decline occur to prevent premature

American Intl. Group

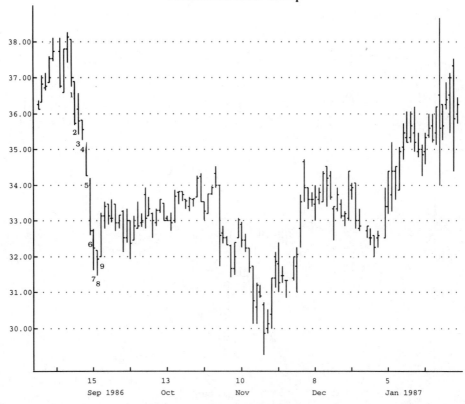

Source: Logical Information Machines, Inc. (LIM), Chicago, IL.

Figure 7.12   Price intersection did not occur on day 8, but it did on day 9 once the price high that day exceeded the low three day's earlier—day 6 in this example.

entry. Conversely, to avoid the problem of early entry in an upside blow-off, an indication that the price brakes have been applied is a necessity. Once the setup has been properly qualified, the next phase of Sequential—the countdown—begins. The setup qualification process, called "intersection," is very easy to understand. Simply stated, intersection requires that the price range of either the eighth or the ninth day of the setup overlap the price activity of any setup day three or more days earlier. In other words, intersection for a buy setup takes place once the high of either day 8 or day 9 of the setup is greater than or equal to the low three, four, five, six, or seven days earlier (see Figures 7.12 and 7.13). On the other hand, intersection

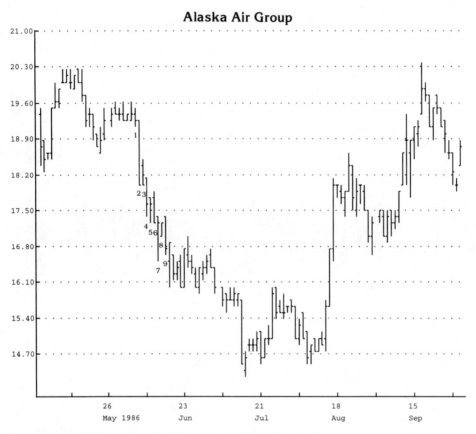

Alaska Air Group

Source: Logical Information Machines, Inc. (LIM), Chicago, IL.

Figure 7.13 Both setups (Figure 7.12 as well) fail to record intersection on day 8 of the setup but they do so on day 9.

for a sell setup occurs once the low of either day 8 or day 9 of the setup is less than or equal to the high three, four, five, six, or seven days earlier (see Figures 7.14 and 7.15). Intersection can also take place in one other instance: if intersection does not occur on day 8 or on day 9 of the setup, then it may occur on any subsequent day, regardless of whether that

Source: Logical Information Machines, Inc. (LIM), Chicago, IL.

Figure 7.14 In both regards—sell setup and buy setup—intersection did not occur on day 8 or day 9 of the setup, but rather on day 13 and day 11, respectively.

day is a continuation of the setup or not. All that is required is that the price intersect the price low three or more days earlier in the case of a buy setup or intersect the price high three or more days earlier in the case of a sell setup. However, in both instances, the countdown phase is postponed until intersection is satisfied (see Figures 7.16 and 7.17).

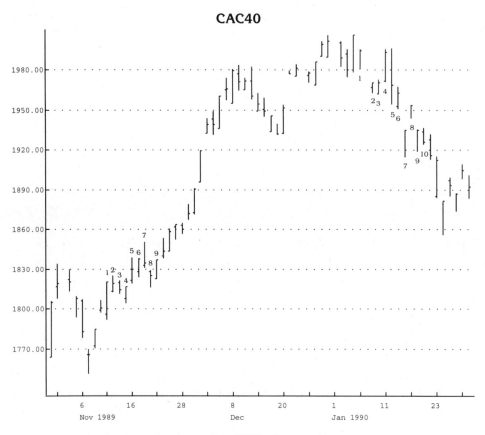

Source: Logical Information Machines, Inc. (LIM), Chicago, IL.

Figure 7.15 Whereas intersection did occur on the sell setup on both day 8 and day 9, for the buy setup it was delayed until day 10.

There are two instances in which the setup can be canceled. They are very simple and straightforward. The most common is a phenomenon called "recycling," which is described in the section on countdown below. The other is related to the closing prices recorded at any time between the completion of the setup and the generation of a signal. More precisely, should a subsequent closing price exceed either the highest intraday high—in the case of a buy setup—or the lowest intraday low—in the case of a sell setup—the setup phase is canceled and it must be reinitialized (see Figures 7.18 and 7.19).

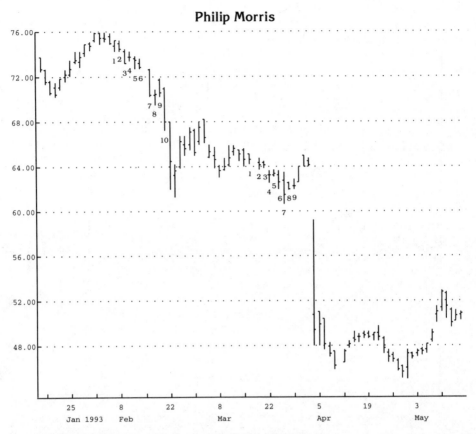

Source: Logical Information Machines, Inc. (LIM), Chicago, IL.

Figure 7.16 The intersection for the first buy setup was postponed until day 10 and countdown does not begin until intersection and the setup are both complete.

Countdown

Once setup has been satisfied, the countdown process begins. Countdown describes the relationship of the close to either the high or the low price two trading days earlier, depending on whether a sell or a buy setup is active (see Figures 7.20 and 7.21). With respect to a pending buy signal, the close must be less than the low two days earlier; with respect to a pending sell signal, the close must be greater than the high two trading days earlier. Once a total of 13 closes less than the low two trading days earlier in the case of a buy, or once a total of 13 closes greater than the high

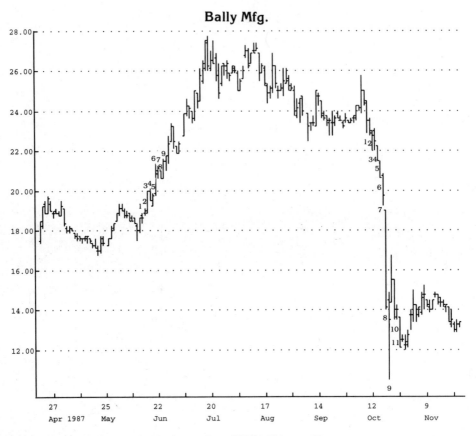

Bally Mfg.

Source: Logical Information Machines, Inc. (LIM), Chicago, IL.

Figure 7.17   The intersection for the sell setup occurred on day 9 of the sell setup. The intersection for the buy setup took place on day 11 of the buy setup.

Soybeans S

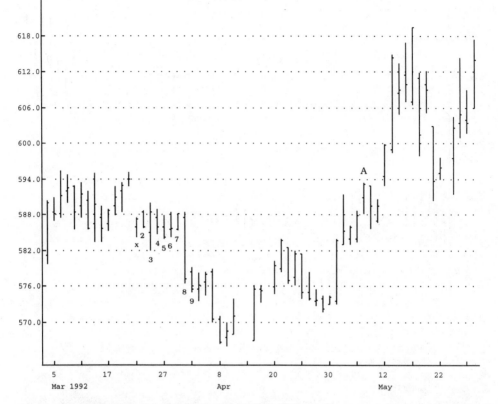

Source: Logical Information Machines, Inc. (LIM), Chicago, IL.

Figure 7.18   Note how close at point A on chart exceeded the highest high of the buy setup in late March counted on the chart.

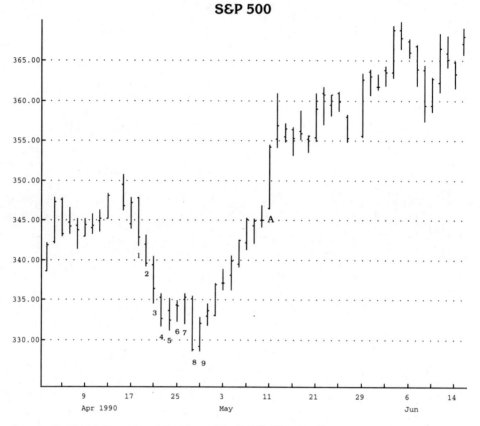

Source: Logical Information Machines, Inc. (LIM), Chicago, IL.

Figure 7.19 In both instances, Figure 7.18, as well as this one, closing price A exceeds the highest intraday high of the buy setup.

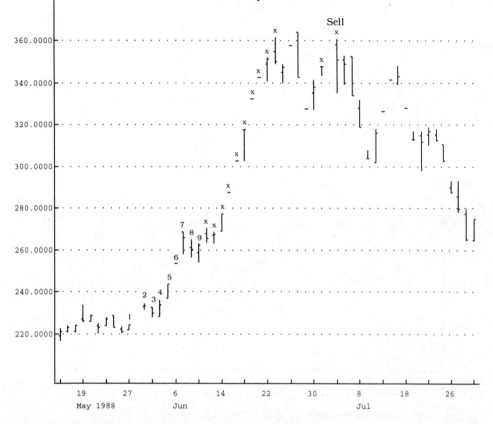

Corn Sept. '88

Source: Logical Information Machines, Inc. (LIM), Chicago, IL.

Figure 7.20   The "X" marked days identify the 13 countdown days recorded upon completion of the sell setup.

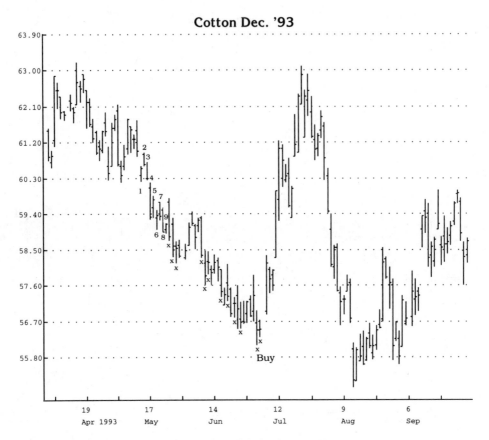

Cotton Dec. '93

Source: Logical Information Machines, Inc. (LIM), Chicago, IL.

Figure 7.21 The "X" marked days identify the 13 countdown days initiated upon completion of the buy setup.

two days earlier in the case of a sell are recorded, a signal is generated. These 13 closes need not occur consecutively; they will occur only rarely, if at all. Once intersection has taken place to validate completion of the setup—and beginning no earlier than day 9 of the setup—the countdown begins. By definition, the countdown period cannot be completed any sooner than 12 days after setup, and that assumes that day 9 qualifies. Typically, however, one might expect 15 to 30 days to lapse between the setup and the completion of countdown (see Figures 7.22 and 7.23).

Two situations that could arise after setup would cancel countdown. The first situation invalidates the original setup and requires the process of setup

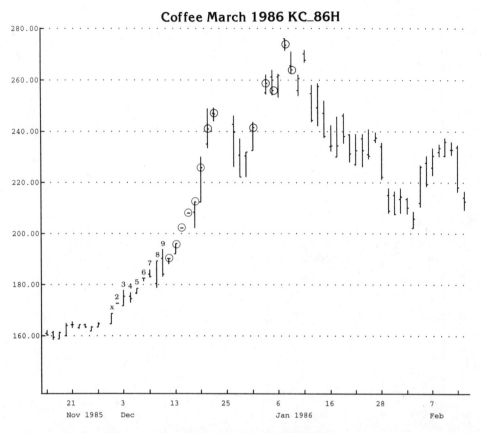

Source: Logical Information Machines, Inc. (LIM), Chicago, IL.

Figure 7.22   Approximately 25 to 30 days lapsed from the initiation of the sell setup to the thirteenth day of sell countdown.

formation to start over. The original setup is negated at any time subsequent to setup, and prior to a signal, a setup in the opposing direction occurs (see Figures 7.24 and 7.25). The second situation does not require additional time to form a new setup, but it does recycle (start over) the countdown phase. In this case, a subsequent setup is formed simultaneously as the countdown process is taking place. This new setup replaces the original setup and is in concert with the original setup, not contradictory (see Figures 7.26 and 7.27). This occurs often and is a function of the market's reevaluating the supply and demand equation and reestablishing the path and the time parameters to the ultimate top or bottom. In both instances, the original setup and the countdown are repealed; in the

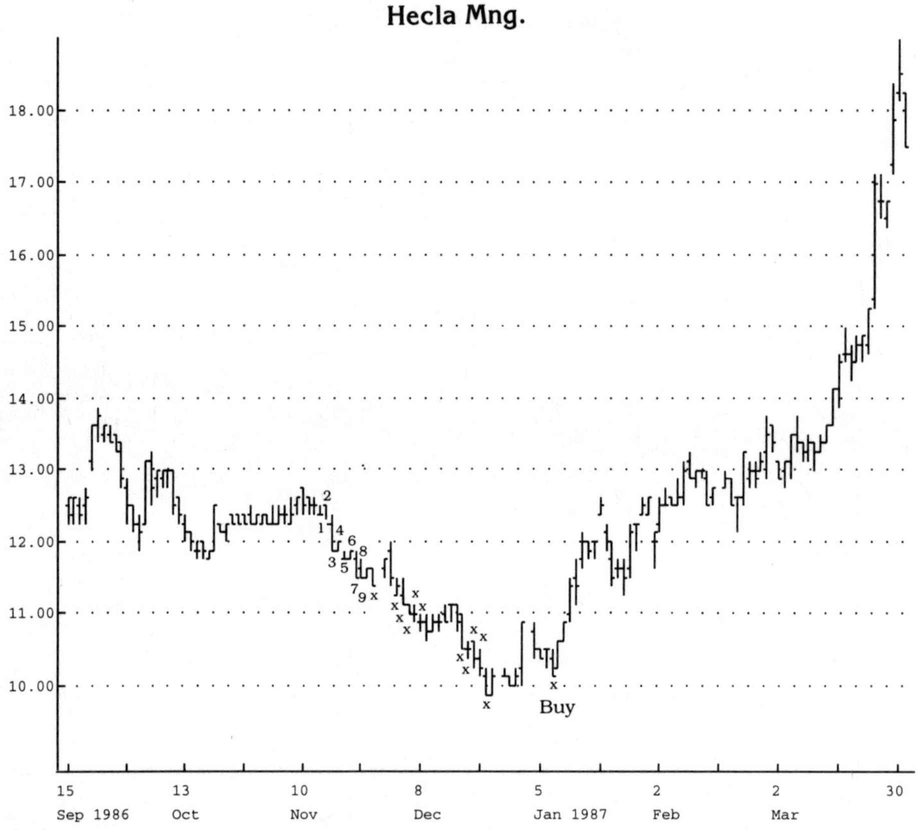

Source: Logical Information Machines, Inc. (LIM), Chicago, IL.

Figure 7.23 Approximately 36 days lapsed from the initiation of the buy setup to the thirteenth and final day of buy countdown.

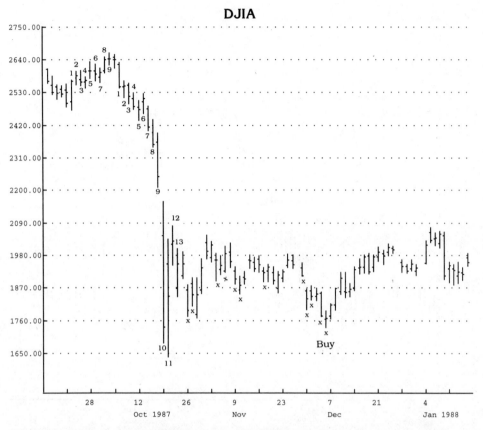

DJIA

Source: Logical Information Machines, Inc. (LIM), Chicago, IL.

Figure 7.24   The ninth day of the sell setup coincided with the exact price high. Subsequently, a buy setup was formed that did not confirm intersection until setup day 13.

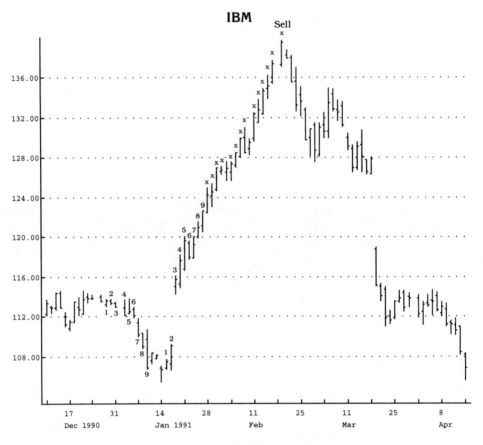

Source: Logical Information Machines, Inc. (LIM), Chicago, IL.

Figure 7.25   The sell setup negated the buy setup that had been formed earlier.

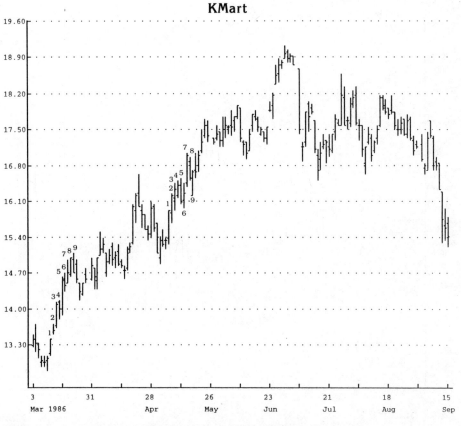

Source: Logical Information Machines, Inc. (LIM), Chicago, IL.

Figure 7.26   The first sell setup was superseded by a second sell setup.

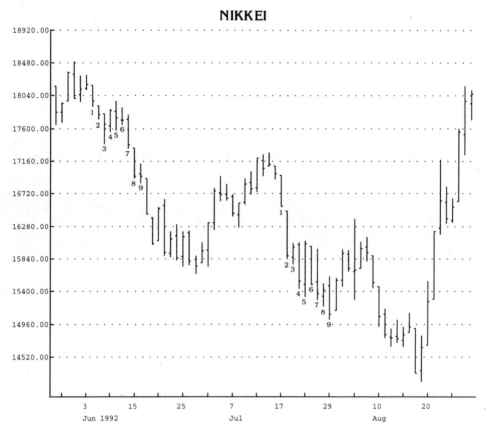

Source: Logical Information Machines, Inc. (LIM), Chicago, IL.

Figure 7.27   The second buy setup negated the first and became active.

second situation, a new setup has been formed through the recycling process.

Now that the setup and the countdown phases have been discussed, three other important aspects of Sequential remain outstanding: (1) the entry, (2) the exit, and (3) the stop loss techniques.

Entry

Three methods are recommended for Sequential entry. The first approach enters the market on the close of the day in which countdown is completed (see Figures 7.28 through 7.31). This is the riskiest entry because the setup can be recycled and the original signal will

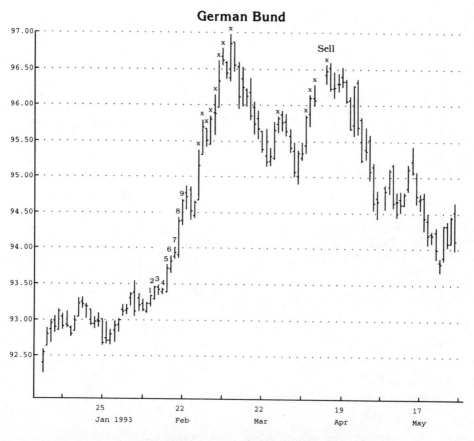

Source: Logical Information Machines, Inc. (LIM), Chicago, IL.

Figure 7.28   Note the sell signal was generated at the high close of the secondary price peak.

evaporate in the process. A new signal cannot be generated until the countdown process has been replayed. Although the potential exists that the trade may produce a loss, it is the only entry of the three that offers the opportunity to buy or to sell at the absolute closing price low or price high.

The second method ensures that price does not recycle and consequently does not forfeit the active signal. However, it requires a price "flip"—a close greater than the close four days earlier in the case of a buy, or a close less than the close four days earlier in the case of a sell (see Figures 7.32 through 7.35). By awaiting the flip, insurance is bought that a setup will not be recycled.

Tribune

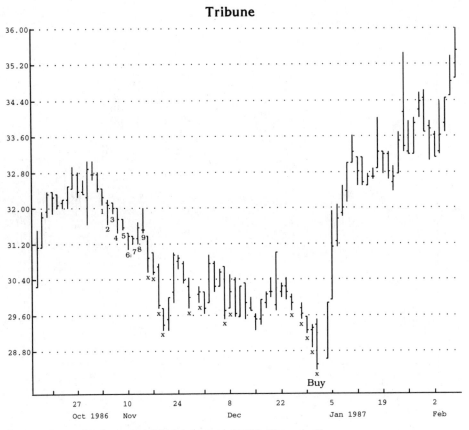

Source: Logical Information Machines, Inc. (LIM), Chicago, IL.

Figure 7.29 The precise low day was identified as the signal day in this example.

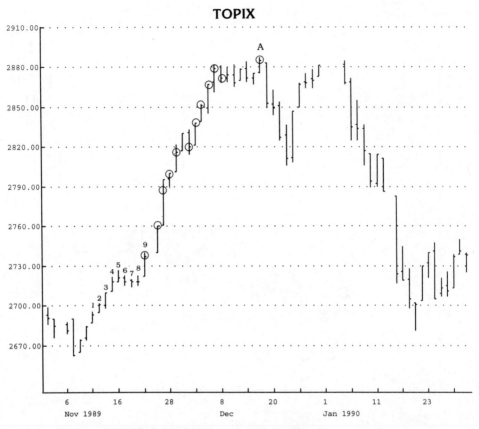

TOPIX

Source: Logical Information Machines, Inc. (LIM), Chicago, IL.

Figure 7.30   Once again the exact high day was the sell day—point A.

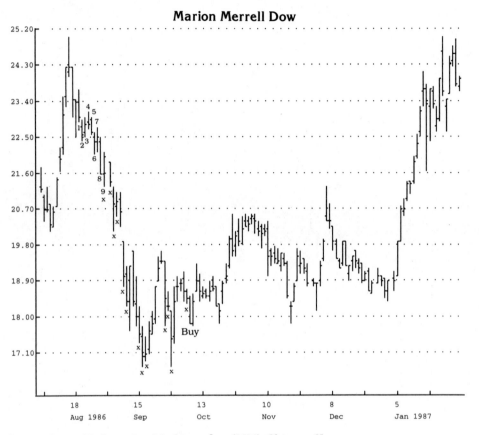

Marion Merrell Dow

Source: Logical Information Machines, Inc. (LIM), Chicago, IL.

Figure 7.31 By executing the trades on the close of the thirteenth day of countdown, ideal entries were selected.

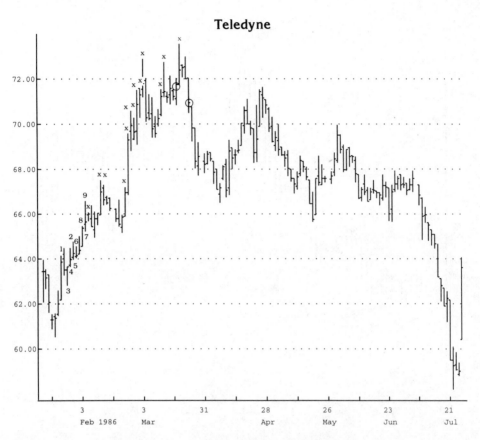

Source: Logical Information Machines, Inc. (LIM), Chicago, IL.

Figure 7.32 Note the "flip" day occurred after the price peak and thirteenth day of countdown, but it confirmed the sell.

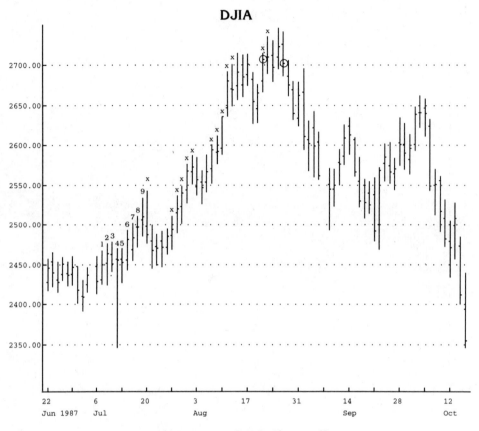

Source: Logical Information Machines, Inc. (LIM), Chicago, IL.

Figure 7.33 See how "flip" day occurred subsequent to actual price high and thirteenth day.

Deutsche Mark

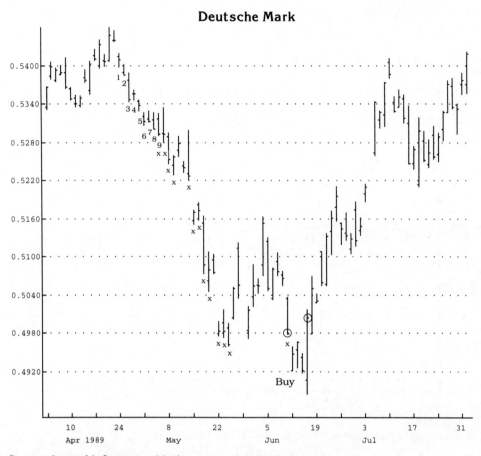

Source: Logical Information Machines, Inc. (LIM), Chicago, IL.

Figure 7.34 Once again confirmation close occurred subsequent to the thirteenth day.

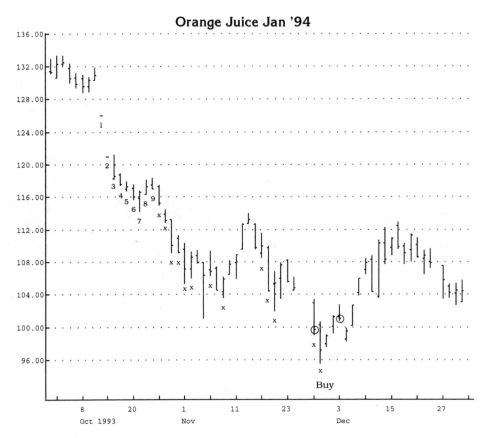

Orange Juice Jan '94

Source: Logical Information Machines, Inc. (LIM), Chicago, IL.

Figure 7.35 By awaiting the initiation of trades until the "flip"—close greater (or less than) the close four days earlier—ideal entries were selected. The entry close is circled and marked A.

③ The final entry technique is to await a two-day range "flip" once the thirteenth day is identified. In other words, once the countdown is completed, buy the first time a subsequent close greater than the high two days earlier occurs or, conversely, sell the first time a subsequent close less than the low two days earlier occurs (see Figures 7.36 through 7.39). This entry perfects the "flip" entry and generally serves as a compromise between entry one and entry two.

Exit

There are two ways in which to exit a trade other than being stopped out of the trade with a loss. The first

Gold

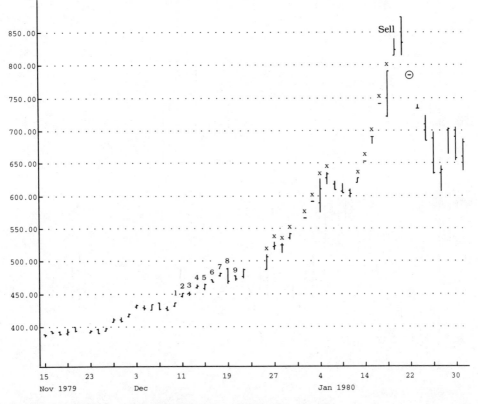

Source: Logical Information Machines, Inc. (LIM), Chicago, IL.

Figure 7.36   See the first close (circled), subsequent to the thirteenth (sell) day, less than the low two days earlier.

method is to liquidate the position once the current setup is completed and price fails to exceed the furthest price level recorded by the most recent inactive setup (see Figures 7.40 and 7.41). This exit assumes that because the trend has not reversed as defined by the point of termination of the active setup failing to exceed the furthest price of the most recent inactive setup, there is a likelihood of an impending reversal and thus the trade should be liquidated.

The other exit also compares the two setups, but in this instance if any price recorded during the current active setup exceeds the furthest price of the inactive setup, then the position is held until a reverse signal is generated.

Hangseng Index

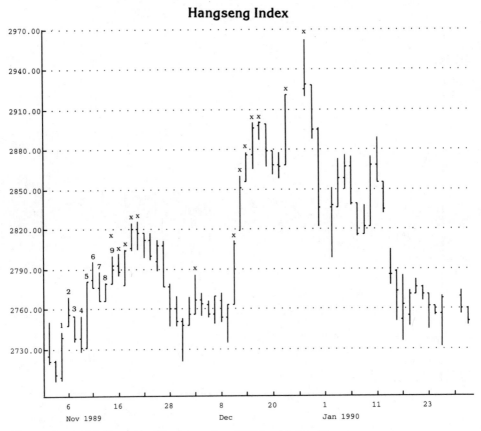

Source: Logical Information Machines, Inc. (LIM), Chicago, IL.

Figure 7.37 In this instance the two-day "flip" confirmation translates into a much less favorable sell entry than was the sale on the peak day—the thirteenth count day.

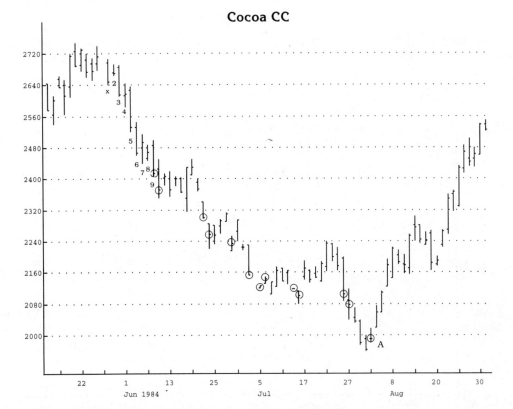

Cocoa CC

Source: Logical Information Machines, Inc. (LIM), Chicago, IL.

Figure 7.38   The entry for the two-day "flip" is close to the signal day in this example.

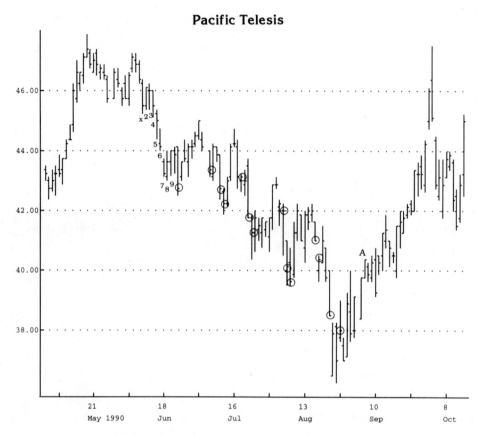

Source: Logical Information Machines, Inc. (LIM), Chicago, IL.

Figure 7.39   Rather than executing the buy on the thirteenth day's close, by awaiting the two-day "flip" confirmation, a less advantageous entry price was recorded.

Stop Loss

The final element to consider is the stop loss. Unfortunately, not all trades are successful. To protect against the chance of failure, a stop loss should be installed. My research suggests that two techniques accomplish this money management goal. Both consider the price range of the lowest range day throughout the entire period of setup and countdown for a buy signal, or the

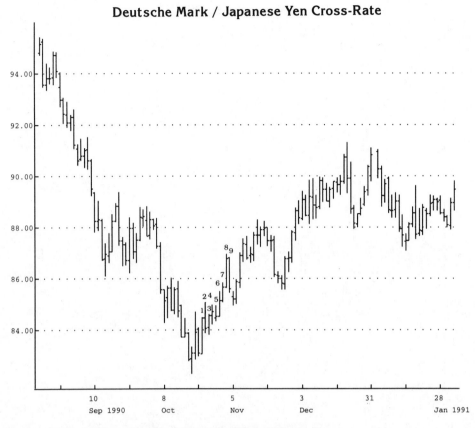

Deutsche Mark / Japanese Yen Cross-Rate

Source: Logical Information Machines, Inc. (LIM), Chicago, IL.

Figure 7.40 As you can see on the chart, the nine up setup identified numerically did not exceed the down setup established beginning 11 days before the October price low.

price range of the highest range day throughout the entire period of setup and countdown for a sell signal. In the case of a buy signal, the true range for the lowest range day is calculated by subtracting the low that day from the high that day or the close the previous day, whichever is greater. The stop loss level is defined as that value subtracted from the low that day (see Figure 7.42). The reverse technique is applied when calculating the stop loss for a sell signal. The true range for the highest range day is calculated by subtracting from the high that day either the low of that day or the close one day earlier, whichever is greater. The stop loss level is defined as that value added to the high that day (see Figure 7.43). In both cases, a

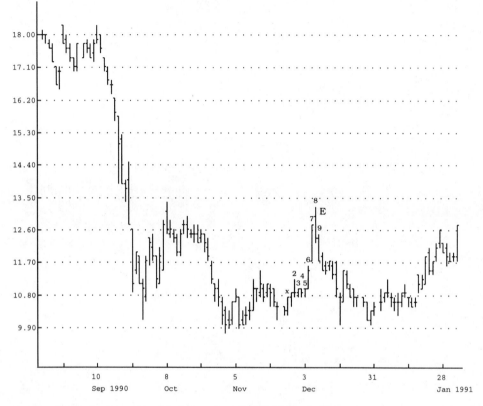

Chase Manhattan Bank CMB

Source: Logical Information Machines, Inc. (LIM), Chicago, IL.

Figure 7.41   The exits are generated if nine consecutive closes greater than the close four days earlier are recorded, a profit is realized, and price does not exceed the setup in the other direction which got you into the trade in the first place.

subsequent close must exceed the calculated values in order to activate a stop loss.

The second stop loss technique is more conservative. In the case of a stop loss for both a buy signal and a sell signal, the same day selection technique is used. Instead of using the true range, however, a stop loss for a buy signal is calculated by subtracting, from the low the difference between the close and the low; a stop loss for a sell signal is calculated by adding to the high the difference between the high and the close. Just as in the previously discussed stop loss, a subsequent close must exceed the stop loss parameters.

Deutsche Mark

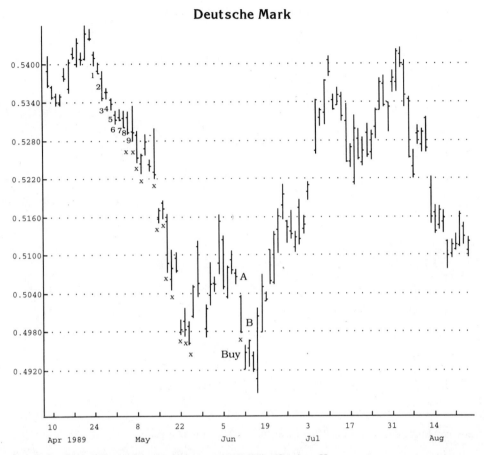

Source: Logical Information Machines, Inc. (LIM), Chicago, IL.

Figure 7.42 Subsequent to the Buy signal, nine consecutive up closes were recorded, and a profitable exit was made.

Both stop losses are based on the assumption that the market expressed a certain degree of pessimism on that extreme price day and to exceed it on a closing basis would constitute a deviation from its price character and consequently jeopardize the signal.

I was convinced that the sequential method worked well when applied to daily data. Occasionally, I would study charts of a shorter time duration than daily. I observed that the sequential technique worked well. Although I don't recommend its use on any time series other than daily, Figure 7.44 demonstrates the successful application of Sequential™ to a minute chart of the Japanese yen.

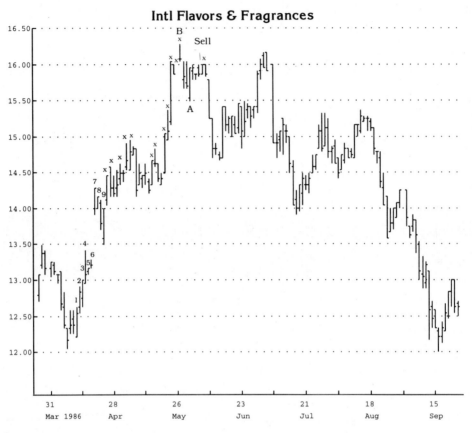

Intl Flavors & Fragrances

Source: Logical Information Machines, Inc. (LIM), Chicago, IL.

Figure 7.43   To establish a stop loss, subtract the true range (Current day's high or close one day ago, whichever is greater − Current day's low or close one day ago, whichever is less). For a buy signal, subtract this value from the lowest day of the setup/countdown period. For a stop loss after a sale, the reverse is done—in this example, the difference between point A—close one day ago—and the high—point B—is added to point B. If price closes above this value, the stop is activated. For a buy stop, everything is reversed.

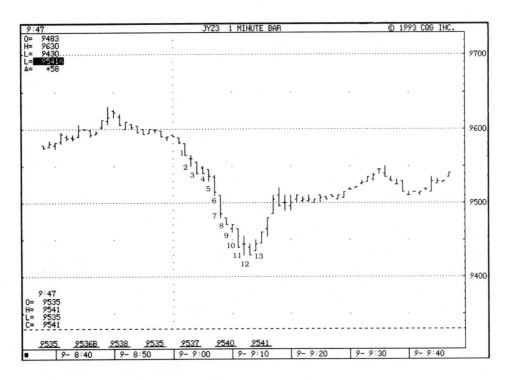

Source: CQG, Glenwood Springs, CO.

Figure 7.44   Note the precision of the 9-13 sequence on identifying the lowest price on the minute chart.

Summary

I have shared with you a technique that appears superficially to be valuable; however, nothing is infallible. Because I was the creator, it is difficult for me to admit the chance of failure. Consequently, it took Paul Tudor Jones and Peter Borish to challenge the method. Their creativity and mindset as floor traders prepared them to accept losses. They queried me regarding the subsequent activity of signals gone awry. Initially, I was insulted by their unwillingness both to focus on the signals and to accept the fact that they would be successful. The price activity of the failures was most instructive. The ones that didn't work were really bad. In a sense, by concentrating on them alone, a trader could enjoy success.

You have been introduced to a powerful tool designed to identify potential turning points in the markets. My experience proves that the technique has universal application to all markets, both foreign and domestic. Its features are its mechanized nature, its long-term perspective, and its ability to fight the prevailing trend. Because of a trader's passion to always be active in the markets, Sequential™ may be considered boring and unappealing. My experience has proven, however, that the most successful traders are at least cognizant of the big picture and take advantage of it. Once again you may be asking yourself why I have given up this valuable brainchild of mine for adoption. I do not view its publication in that context, however. I see it as an opportunity for you to do some babysitting for me while I pursue other market avenues of interest. In addition, in recent years I have introduced two noteworthy enhancements to this basic approach which I have not discussed. I am confident that as you acquire proficiency with this technique, you will also be equipped to make similar improvements.

Chapter

Gaps

A market psychologist will confirm the fact that emotions such as fear and greed play a significant part in determining price swings in the market. In fact, many market letter writers earn a living by measuring these sentiments and making recommendations based on their assessment of the collective opinions of the trading masses. There is a belief that in order to be successful in the market, a trader must buy when everyone is selling and sell when everyone is buying. In general, this is a valid observation because the consensus is generally wrong. Simply stated, logic dictates that as price moves higher the number of potential buyers is depleted until there remains, figuratively speaking, only the "last buyer" left to buy; consequently, by default, price declines. Conversely, as price declines, the number of prospective sellers diminishes until there remains only the "last seller" left to sell; consequently, by default, price advances. Just consider the roles of the specialists and the floor traders. Both provide liquidity to the markets by selling strength and by buying weakness. At the same time, they are always battling the trend and they make a comfortable living doing so. Although the most pronounced dislocations typically occur at the opening, these traders are afforded an advantage because they are responsible for setting the opening price. Opening price moves that exceed the previous day's close and fail to be filled by the close of trading are called either price gaps or price laps. Gaps occur when a particular day's price high or low fails to intersect the previous day's price high or low. Laps occur when the price high or low intersects the previous day's high or low but not the previous day's close (see Figures 8.1 and 8.2). Although much discussion in the past has been devoted to the topic of gaps, most of the research has been lacking. For the sake of ease of presentation, I will label both gaps and laps as gaps. My research

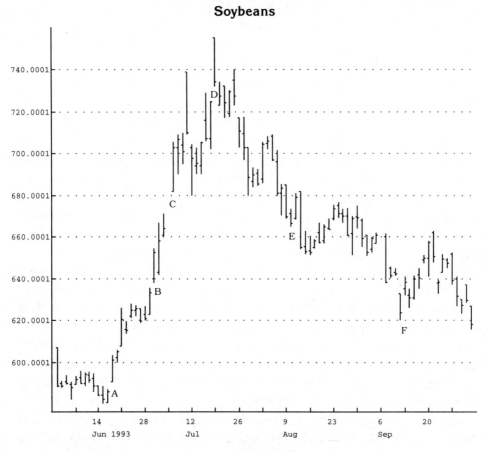

Source: Logical Information Machines, Inc. (LIM), Chicago, IL.

Figure 8.1 Points A, B, and C are upside gaps: the price lows do not overlap with the previous day's highs. Points E and F are considered upside laps: the price lows overlap the previous day's highs, but do not overlap the previous day's closes.

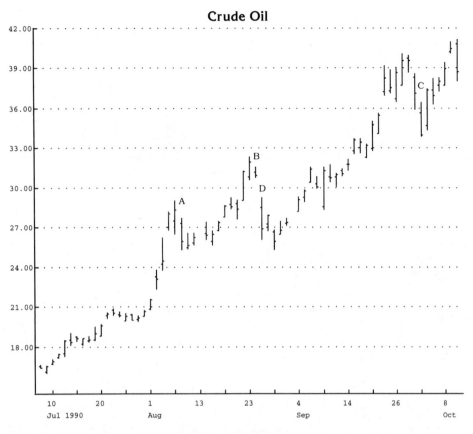

Crude Oil

Source: Logical Information Machines, Inc. (LIM), Chicago, IL.

Figure 8.2 Points A, B, and C are downside laps: the price highs intersect the previous day's lows, but do not intersect the previous day's closes. Point D is a downside gap: the price high does not intersect the previous day's low.

regarding gaps is unconventional and sheds light on a different perspective in which to view them.

An old market adage teaches that all price gaps are filled. I'm certain that a seller of Chrysler stock in the 1930s will dispute this claim, as will a seller of the Dow Jones Industrial Average in early 1975 (see Figure 8.3). To date, neither gap has been filled. These are prime examples of how market folklore has been accepted and has been promoted as doctrine. All gaps are not filled, and even those that are will sometimes leave the trader poorer by the time they are. In my studies of gaps, I have made some worthwhile observations. Once again I have elected to draw my own

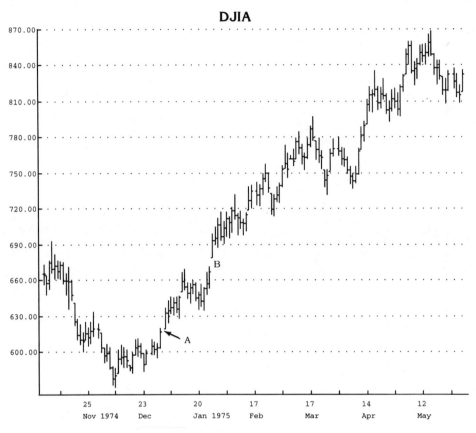

Source: Logical Information Machines, Inc. (LIM), Chicago, IL.

Figure 8.3   The lap of January 2, 1975 (A), and the gap of January 27, 1975 (B), were never filled, contradicting the notion that all gaps (laps) are filled.

conclusions and ignore those misconceptions widely held as fact.

Most price gaps are filled within a few days of their occurrence. Should you accept this as fact, however, I assure you that just when you initiate a trade, it will not work. To reduce the likelihood of this event occurring, I observed those instances when price gaps were not filled for an extended period of time. What I found interesting was the fact that if gaps are precipitated by minor news events, they are usually filled quickly, even the same day. If the gap is associated with a major, unexpected announcement or with no news whatsoever, it is more likely to be legitimate and remain unfilled for an extended period of time. Taken together with the following conditions more substance and significance can be assigned to a gap.

As was mentioned earlier, emotions are generally a major contributor to a price gap. When I looked to identify instances when this influence is either eliminated or muted, I uncovered four:

1. When news is announced over a weekend or, ideally, over a long holiday weekend;

2. When news is either decidedly negative or positive and a price gap occurs unexpectedly in the opposite direction;

3. When both a period of more than 11 days has elapsed since the gap occurred and when the close of day 8, day 9, or day 10 after the gap is the extreme close since the gap day;

4. When volume on the opening is light and continues afterward, suggesting a shortage of either supply in an upside move or demand in a downside move.

Over an extended period of time such as a weekend, a trader is able to evaluate events more rationally than overnight. Removed from the office or news releases, he is able to detach himself, temper his emotions, and make cooler, more calculated decisions. For those reasons, Monday—or, in the case of long weekends, Tuesday—gaps assume a special significance (see Figures 8.4 and 8.5). Furthermore, committee meetings are generally held on Mondays and at that time all the facts are dissected thoroughly, thus providing a sense of premeditation, deliberation, and forethought, rather than emotion, to a decision. I am particularly aware of gap price activity on Mondays and often review weekly charts; Monday gaps—on the first trading day of the week—are easily identified. By incorporating the other gap observations mentioned,

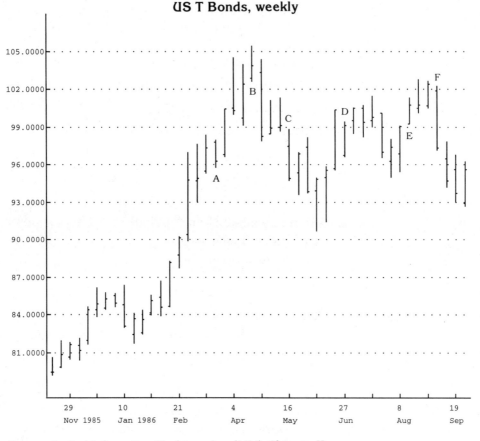

US T Bonds, weekly

Source: Logical Information Machines, Inc. (LIM), Chicago, IL.

Figure 8.4 By using a weekly chart, Monday gaps (laps) are identified easily. They occur at points A, B, C, D, E, and F.

such as volume and time considerations, authenticity can be further confirmed and impact can be anticipated.

If a particular event has been anticipated for a period of time and a number of false starts regarding the release of this information have occurred prior to its actual release, then there exists a good chance that the news has already been discounted. On those rare occasions, the opening price may actually gap in the other direction and the gap remains unfilled (see Figure 8.6). Such an event would be totally unexpected and would carry significant implications—as well as opportunity—for the alert trader.

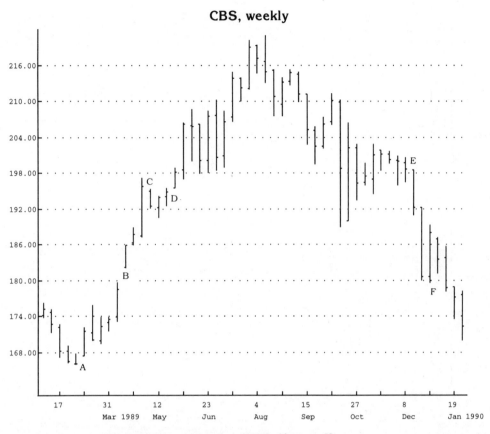

CBS, weekly

Source: Logical Information Machines, Inc. (LIM), Chicago, IL.

Figure 8.5 By using a weekly chart, Monday gaps (laps) are identified easily. They occur at points (A, B, C, D, E, and F).

Because the expectation is that most gaps are soon filled, I examined those instances when a gap remained unfilled for an extended period of time. My conclusion was, essentially, if a gap is not filled within the ensuing 11 trading days after it appears, price usually continues to move in the direction of the gap until its momentum is exhausted. This observation is valid with the following exception—the closing price of day 8, day 9, or day 10 after the gap must be the most extreme close day since the gap day (see Figures 8.7 and 8.8).

Volume is an important factor when analyzing gaps. Heavy volume on a gap opening is generally news-inspired and short-lived. On the other hand, my

DJIA

Source: Logical Information Machines, Inc. (LIM), Chicago, IL.

Figure 8.6   Because of the Middle-East oil disruption and the threat of U.S. war involvement, expectations were for the stock market to decline. Unexpectedly, the DJIA rallied sharply beginning with a upside price gap (A).

research suggests that light volume gaps are durable and appear as a thief in the night—unexpectedly, without any warning whatsoever. Their significance is often dismissed because they come with no fanfare or hoopla. In these cases, relatively speaking, the volume is not exceptional and the price change on the opening is nominal. However, when these particular ingredients are packaged together, the impact they supply is powerful indeed. A trader should be alert to their occurrences and be prepared to take advantage of them.

Gaps have been relegated to the trading doghouse. Although their presence is obvious, no one has attempted to justify and explain their existence. The

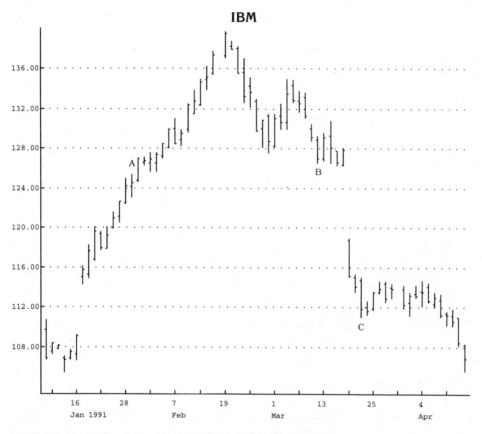

IBM

Source: Logical Information Machines, Inc. (LIM), Chicago, IL.

Figure 8.7 The close on day 8 subsequent to the gap was an extreme close (A)—greater than all previous 7 closes—thus qualifying the gap and suggesting the trend would continue. The same signal in reverse was indicated by the downside lap, which was confirmed 10 days later by an extreme close (B). The same indication was given 8, 9, and 10 days after the downside gap at point C.

descriptions and lame explanations offered by conventional analysts regarding specific gaps, as well as the classification of varieties such as "breakaway," "mid-," and "exhaustion" gaps, are lacking excuses and often without merit. Taken in the context of the subject matter presented in Chapters 1 and 2, which discuss TD Line breakouts and retracements, however, gaps assume a significance not revealed before. By being aware of the characteristics of gaps, a trader can be better prepared and equipped to handle their implications and turn them to his profitable advantage.

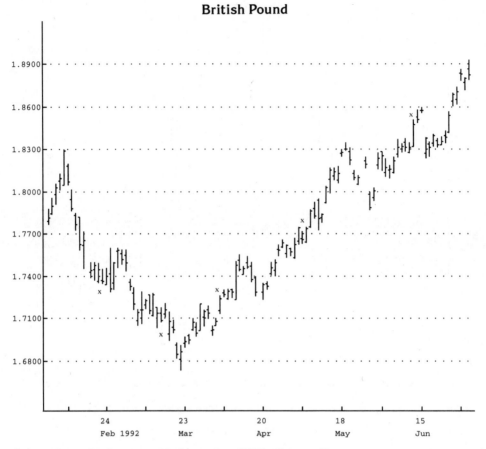

British Pound

Source: Logical Information Machines, Inc. (LIM), Chicago, IL.

Figure 8.8 The downside and upside gaps and laps were confirmed by extreme closes 8, 9, and 10 days later.

Chapter

Daily Range
Projections

In the early 1980s, I appeared regularly on Financial News Network prior to the daily opening and announced the projected price ranges for various markets. The formula presented below is an enhanced version of the one I used to make these projections. It is the product of many hours of research, and its interpretation is important in defining short-term price movement.

My research has shown that tomorrow's price range is influenced by the relationship between the current day's price close versus the current day's price open. There are three possible relationships between the close today and the open today:

1. The close today is less than the open today;

2. The close today is greater than the open today;

3. The close today is equal to the open today.

If relationship 1 exists, I use the following formula to project the range for the following day:

$$(\text{High today} + \text{Low today} + \text{Close today} + \text{Low today})/ 2 = X$$

Tomorrow's projected high = X − Today's low

Tomorrow's projected low = X − Today's high

If relationship 2 exists, I revise the formula as follows:

$$(\text{High today} + \text{Low today} + \text{Close today} + \text{High today})/ 2 = X$$

Tomorrow's projected high = X − Today's low

Tomorrow's projected low = X − Today's high

If relationship 3 occurs, I make the following adjustments:

$$(\text{High today} + \text{Low today} + \text{Close today} + \text{Close today})/ 2 = X$$

Tomorrow's projected high = X − Today's low

Tomorrow's projected low = X − Today's high

These values merely provide a benchmark for the ensuing day's price activity. I recommend that the figures be used as follows: If price opens within the projected price range and you are a day trader, anticipate resistance above the projected high and expect support at the projected low. More importantly, should price open outside the projected range—above the projected high or below the projected low—the supply–demand balance has shifted significantly enough to imply that the short-term price trend will continue in the direction of the opening breakout. Two options exist for the short-term trader if such a breakout occurs:

1. Ignore the projected ranges for the day;

2. Adjust the value for the projected low to just below the projected high in the case of an upside breakout; conversely, revise the value for

the projected high to just above the projected
low in the case of a downside breakout.

Although the performance results achieved by
this formula in the past have been respectable because it has established realistic parameters for the
following day's price activity, I make no guarantee
that this performance will continue.

For purposes of illustration, Table 9.1 shows the
range predictions for Soybeans March 1994.

Table 9.1   Soybeans March 1994

	Actual				Projected	
	Open	High	Low	Close	High	Low
1/26/94				700.25		
1/27	704.0	704.5	693.5	696.5		
1/28	694.5	696.0	683.0	683.75	700.5	689.5
1/31	683.75	687.25	681.5	686.75	685.75	677.0
2/1	686.5	690.75	686.0	687.0	690.0	684.25
2/2	*684.5	684.75	675.0	683.5	691.25	686.5

*Open below projected low—revise projected high to level of original projected low.

Chapter

10

Rate of Change

On numerous occasions, I've been approached by college students who wanted to know what courses would best prepare them for a career in the stock market or the futures market. Recalling my own educational experience—liberal arts, study abroad, graduate school of business, and law school—I invariably respond *not* to follow in my footsteps. In the trading profession, what is most obvious is often most obviously wrong. I grant that fundamentals or the perception of them dictate the long-term trend in markets; however, over shorter time periods, the recognition of these fundamental developments might be ignored or overlooked. As a result, the price of a security may either remain dormant or contradict reason and logic. Effective market timing techniques help alert the user to the appropriate times when the price may be disposed to respond favorably or unfavorably. The identification of these precise points in time is accomplished by measuring both supply/demand and market sentiment.

My techniques concentrate on basic economics and mass psychology. Consequently, I believe an understanding of these two areas of knowledge is vital to success—the former for purpose of measuring supply and demand and the latter for evaluating the emotionalism of the market.

Of the highly educated professors you know, how many have been successful traders? I would venture to guess: not very many. Their lack of success is no reflection on their intelligence; over the long run, their fundamental expectations *can* make them successful investors. Short-term trading, however, is a full-time profession, and markets do not always operate rationally. In fact, my experience suggests that an inverse correlation exists between education and short-term trading success. Much of the information taught in business school is of a fundamental nature and does not address the key emotions dictating short-term price movement—fear and greed. Markets are efficient, and once information is released the discount process begins immediately defining the impact of this news. In many instances, price movements are exaggerated because of dynamics outside the arena of fundamental analysis, such as stop losses, systems' trading signals, margin calls, and so on. Consequently, the immediate price movement may contradict all logical expectations. Figuratively speaking, I have often said that price continues to advance until the last buyer has bought, and price continues to decline until the last seller has sold, and that this sequence of events accounts for perceived illogical market responses.

Many years ago, I experimented with a price comparison that incorporated market timing and market sentiment. For the most part, I applied this approach to major market indexes and to futures markets, rather than individual stocks, because the likelihood of price declining to zero was a real possibility with a stock.

Specifically, I divided the current price of the security by the price of the security one year earlier. Other time periods may work better, depending on the market, but I wanted to cover the same time periods for all markets.

From the chart prepared for each market, I can design overbought/oversold bands that have historically defined areas of low-risk buy and sell levels. For a monthly perspective, the chart is updated monthly;

for a weekly perspective, the chart is updated weekly; and for a daily perspective, it can be updated daily. In each instance, however, the close is compared with the close one year earlier.

One major benefit is derived from this approach. If the market is in an oversold condition, buys based on another shorter-term system can be generated. Conversely, if the market is in an overbought condition, sells based on another shorter-term system can be generated. In any case, even as an indicator unto itself, this relationship measures the level of emotion associated with price moves and visually displays how similar movements have evolved in the past. The degree of advance or of decline can be evaluated, and the extent of movement within overbought/oversold zones can be examined and compared. In fact, price activity recorded a year ago dictates current price movement by defining extreme parameters associated with historical turning points.

Figures 10.1 through 10.15 are examples of charts used for this type of comparative analysis.

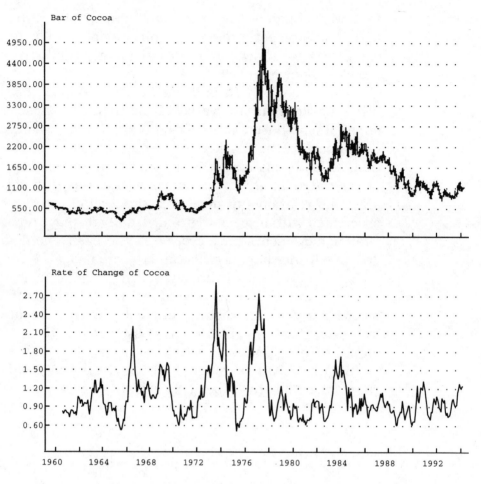

Source: Logical Information Machines, Inc. (LIM), Chicago, IL.

Figure 10.1 One-year rate of change, cocoa monthly.

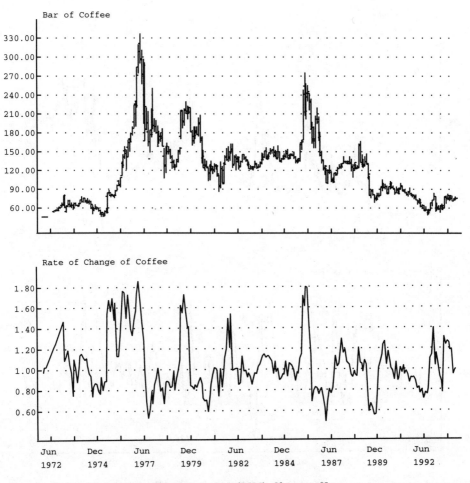

Bar of Coffee

Rate of Change of Coffee

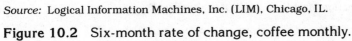

Source: Logical Information Machines, Inc. (LIM), Chicago, IL.

Figure 10.2   Six-month rate of change, coffee monthly.

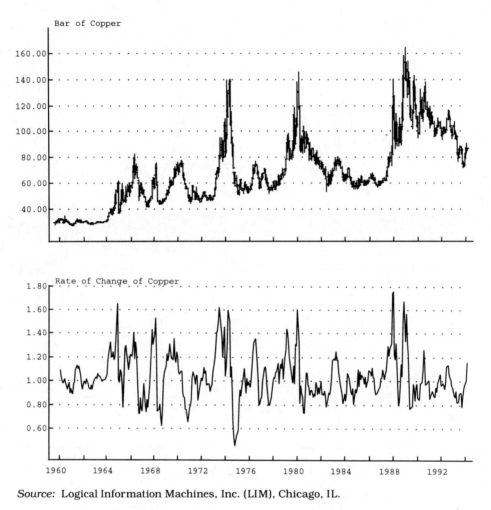

Source: Logical Information Machines, Inc. (LIM), Chicago, IL.

Figure 10.3   Six-month rate of change, copper monthly.

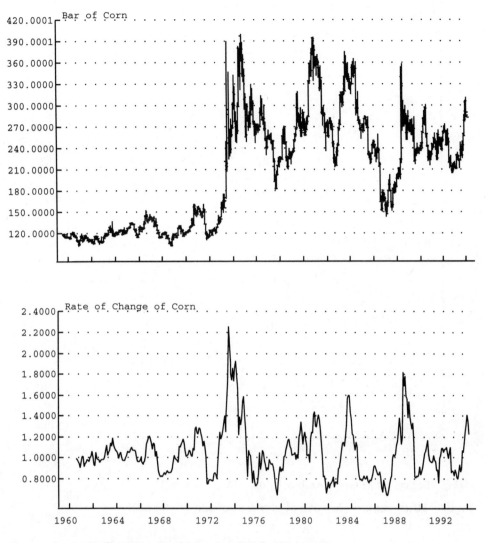

Source: Logical Information Machines, Inc. (LIM), Chicago, IL.

Figure 10.4   One-year rate of change, corn monthly.

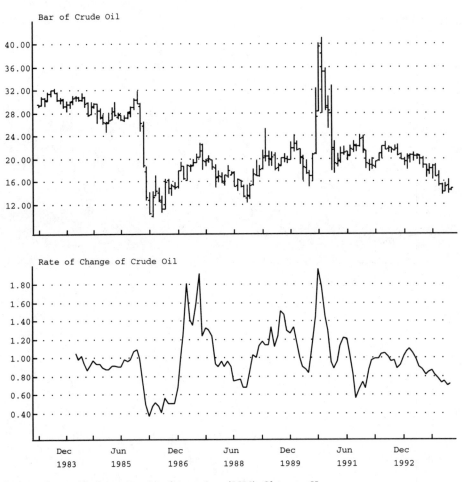

Source: Logical Information Machines, Inc. (LIM), Chicago, IL.

Figure 10.5   One-year rate of change, crude oil monthly.

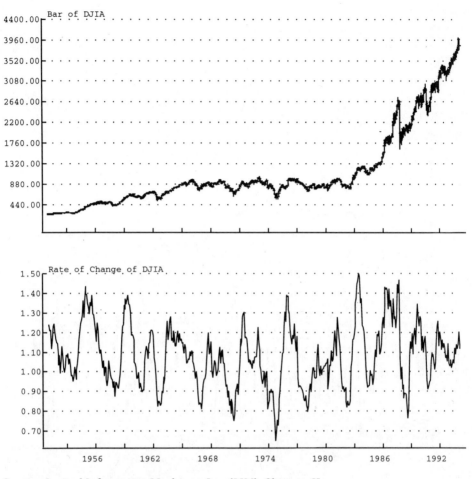

Source: Logical Information Machines, Inc. (LIM), Chicago, IL.

Figure 10.6 One-year rate of change, DJIA monthly.

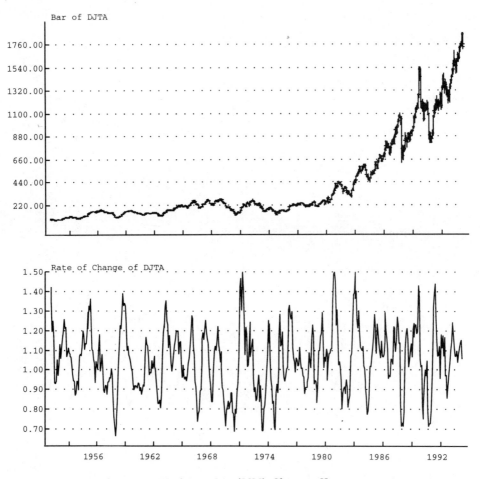

Source: Logical Information Machines, Inc. (LIM), Chicago, IL.

Figure 10.7   One-year rate of change, DJTA monthly.

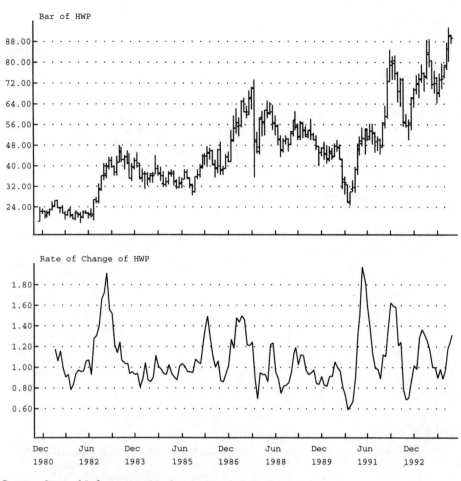

Source: Logical Information Machines, Inc. (LIM), Chicago, IL.

Figure 10.8   Six-month rate of change, Hewlett-Packard monthly.

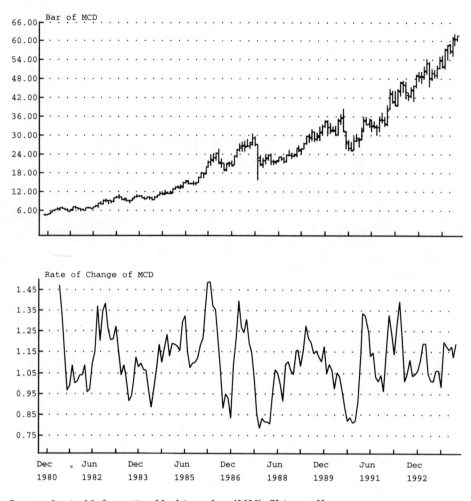

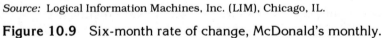

Source: Logical Information Machines, Inc. (LIM), Chicago, IL.

Figure 10.9   Six-month rate of change, McDonald's monthly.

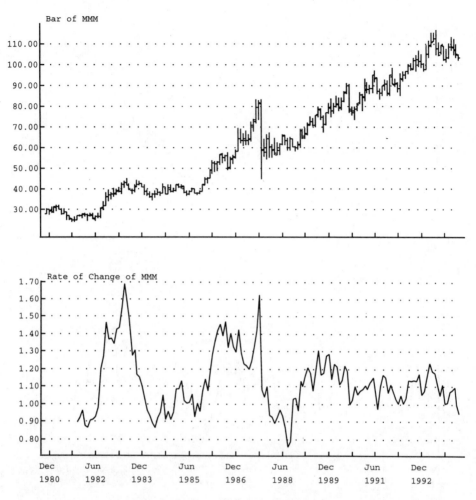

Source: Logical Information Machines, Inc. (LIM), Chicago, IL.

Figure 10.10 One-year rate of change, Minnesota Mining Corporation monthly.

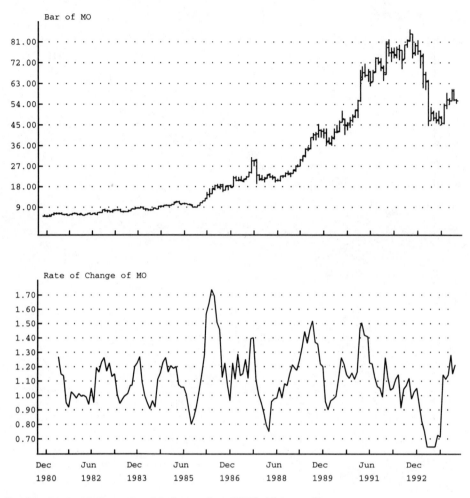

Source: Logical Information Machines, Inc. (LIM), Chicago, IL.

Figure 10.11   Six-month rate of change, Philip Morris Corporation.

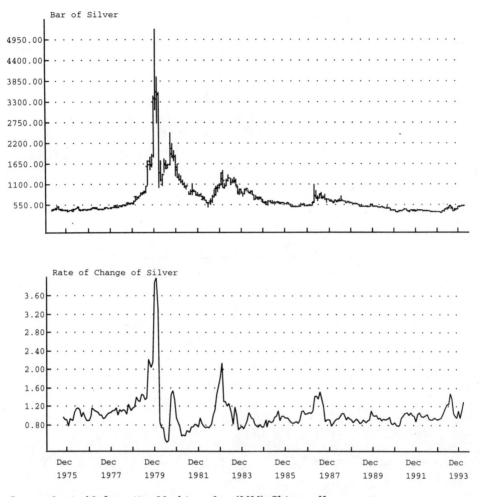

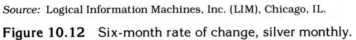

Source: Logical Information Machines, Inc. (LIM), Chicago, IL.

Figure 10.12   Six-month rate of change, silver monthly.

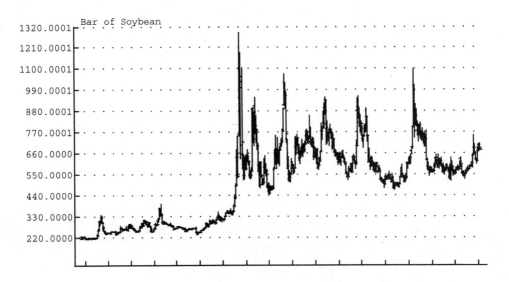

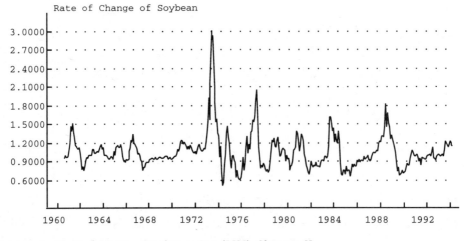

Source: Logical Information Machines, Inc. (LIM), Chicago, IL.

Figure 10.13 One-year rate of change, soybean monthly.

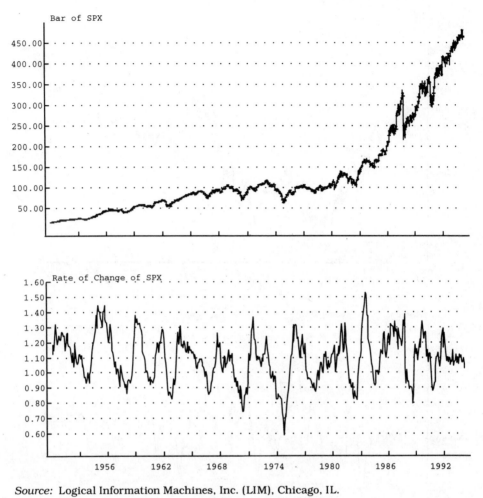

Source: Logical Information Machines, Inc. (LIM), Chicago, IL.

Figure 10.14 Six-month rate of change, cash S&P monthly.

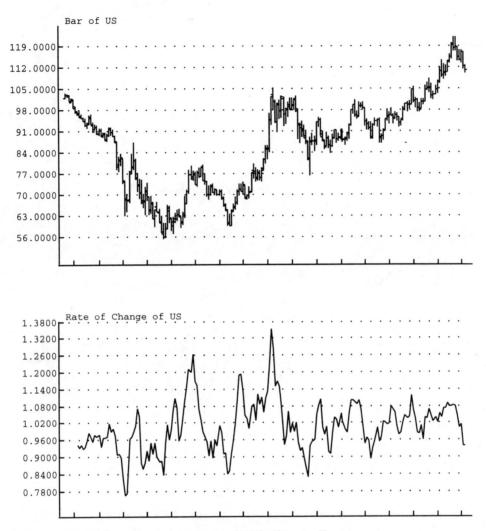

Source: Logical Information Machines, Inc. (LIM), Chicago, IL.

Figure 10.15   Six-month rate of change, U.S. T-bonds monthly.

Chapter

11

Equities

Throughout this book, I have presented numerous methods and strategies designed to decode the market puzzle. My experience suggests that these techniques can be applied to all markets equally well. Whether your specific interest lies in the area of cash currency, commodity, fixed income, or stock trading, the applications and the results should be comparable. Because of the variations in market composition, however, composite indexes may vary from one market to another. In this chapter, I intend to highlight various trading strategies I have created and have applied to both individual stocks and the stock market.

New Issues—Initial Public Offerings

For many years, I have observed a similar trading pattern for most newly issued stocks. I have been particularly sensitive to the trading activity of these new issues because I was in charge of trading these stocks when I first entered the investment business over 23 years ago. Although nothing in the investment business is for certain, and most techniques, following a period during which they work exceptionally well, undergo a period of erosion and disinterest, this method seems to have successfully withstood the rigors of various market environments and of time. Whether the climate for public offerings is hot or cold, this technique on balance seems to work, although the degree of success seems to be influenced somewhat by the overall market.

Typically, once a new issue begins to trade, I look for the following characteristics regardless of the price at which the public offering is completed. Often, price will either advance or at least move sideways for a few days. The reason for this price movement is that the selling syndicate that initially offered the shares to the public for sale supports the price of the stock for a period of time. If the original offering is priced conservatively, the syndicate's price support activity is not as critical. However, if the underwriter attempts to raise the maximum amount for the selling company, it may stretch the market to the point where prospective buyers believe it to be too expensive; price then declines. In any case, the syndicate usually is able to muster enough buying to support the offering price. In fact, I have heard of some instances in which the underwriter has insured the absence of supply by failing to compensate its brokers with commissions when their clients "flipped" a new issue—bought the offering and immediately liquidated once trading began, which forced the syndicate to buy it at the syndicate bid.

Whether the stock's price remains above the public market offering price or not, there is a tendency for price to retreat or move sideways for two to four weeks after the first two to three days of trading. Then, at about the time when most of the people originally interested in the offering become distracted, a new, more subdued surge in buying generally appears. To fine-tune the arrival of this secondary interest, I often review specific items regarding the offering. I make an effort to obtain information regarding the size of the public offering, the name of the underwriter(s), the size of the selling syndicate, the number of market makers in the stock if on National Association of Securities Dealers Automated Quotations (NASDAQ), the amount of stock the underwriter(s) will place with investors, the volume and dollar-weighted volume for each day since the offering, and so on. This is not to say that the price activity will not conform to the one I anticipated if these items are lacking; rather, I use these criteria to market-time entries, as well as to reinforce my expectations.

Once I have information regarding the number of shares offered for sale, I attempt to learn how much stock the underwriter has placed in the hands of buyers. Underwriters often attempt to place the stock in strong hands—in other words, with buyers who are prepared to hold the stock for a period of time rather than liquidate once trading begins. They accomplish this by denying commissions to the broker if the stock is flipped (sold immediately) at a loss. Generally, the underwriter is obligated to support the stock at the offering price level for a period of time, and may not want to increase its inventory. Consequently, I make the assumption that the stock held by the underwriters and their customers should not be a factor in the market for a period of time. Next, I calculate the balance of stock offered by the other syndicate members. With that figure in mind, I observe the trading volume for the ensuing days. As a rule of thumb, once the syndicate members' stock has been turned over two times, the upside move should resume.

Other items, such as the price of the stock and the exchange on which it will be listed, are incidental factors that should also be considered. Many institutions are precluded from buying a stock that does not appear on an approved list. Frequently, a stock cannot be included on the approved list if it is not priced above $10. Most reputable new issues are traded on NASDAQ, with a few exceptions that qualify for the listed exchanges. Margin requirements associated with these exchanges are important considerations as well.

Other factors, such as the lifting of the "quiet period" and the removal of major restrictions, often revitalize interest in the stock. Furthermore, a primary consideration is the subject of supply. As mentioned in Chapter 1, many investors who own a stock at a loss will sell once they break even. In the case of a recent new issue, there is no supply because there are no buyers with a loss.

The various factors I review when I consider a new issue should not be confused with the basic tendency inherent in stocks offered in the new issue aftermarket. A noticeable pattern to advance appears three to five weeks after the offering. I suggest that, in order to be alerted to potential trading candidates, you subscribe to a chart service such as O'Neill's Daily Graphs, which monitors the daily price history of many of these stocks just after public trading begins to follow this price behavior.

Buy-Outs

I have been in the investment business for a long enough time to witness all the fads and market concepts that are imaginable. The era of corporate takeovers was a thrill for me. Fortunately, the supply–demand models I had created were installed and were being successfully used prior to the advent of this period. Initially, my work would alert me to those situations in which aggressive buying was taking place. Most technicians are parasites and require no fundamental justification for their market activities, so I assumed that positive fundamental developments had precipitated this demand. I was soon to learn that a pattern had developed that correctly predicted pending buy-outs. At last count, between 1978 and 1982, more than 32 acquisitions were correctly forecast. I even had the gall to notify corporate presidents and announce that their companies were being acquired. In fact, I was described by one journalist as the "grim reaper." The techniques are described in Chapters 5 and 7, which discuss accumulation/distribution and Sequential© respectively. Both methods combined were sufficiently sensitive to identify these opportunities. In this chapter, my goal is to share information I acquired from experience to further validate acquisition candidates.

Having played basketball, I was never satisfied with the easy lay-up. When I was put in a lay-up situation, I often passed the ball or made an effort to score with a more difficult shot. The same strategy applied to inside information and potential buy-outs. Not only did I prefer to make the process a challenge but I also was confident that by the time pending rumors of buy-outs were widespread and nothing was announced formally, the rumors were more than likely bogus. I tried to explain this to others, but they were unwilling to listen. I did much research to convince them with logic and with examples.

In the early 1970s, there were occasional buy-out rumors. Most legitimate instances demonstrated a similar pattern. I noticed that a surge in price volume was followed by a respite period of typically just over six months. I came to respect this pattern; under the tax laws at that time, long-term capital gains required a holding period of six months. Furthermore, the governmental agencies were not actively involved in prosecuting traders for insider activity. Consequently, I was always aware of rumors from reliable sources and I advised others that, typically, the official announcement was more than likely forthcoming much later because the insiders were probably still in the process of accumulating stock personally—even though I never capitalized on this fact myself. At the same time, the acquiring company was careful not to accumulate more than the maximum allowable percentage of the shares outstanding before the government required a formal acquisition announcement.

After the tax law was changed to abolish the six-month holding period requirement, other factors that served to confirm rumors of a buy-out were tested and were applied successfully. My belief was that once the rumors were received by the lowest common trading denominator—the public—and still nothing was formally released, more than likely they were nothing more than rumors. To prove this fact to others, I conducted the following exercise. First, I researched and confirmed the total shares outstanding. Next, I multiplied the number of shares outstanding by 5 percent to arrive at a benchmark. In turn, I multiplied this figure by a factor of 5. Because the Securities and Exchange Commission (SEC) requires any shareholder accumulating in excess of 5 percent of a company to divulge this information, I assumed that for every share a potential buyer accumulated, four shares were being bought by others. Were a rumor proven to be fact, then the critical 5 percent ownership would most likely be completed by the time 25 percent of the shares outstanding had been traded. This particular filter process served me well in convincing others to avoid disasters.

Another important observation I have made throughout the years relates to the price activity displayed by a stock which has been "put into acquisition play" by the release of a statement from the acquiring company. Specifically, once the announcement is made and it is a cash—as opposed to a stock—purchase offer and the price of the shares immediately trade at or above the acquisition price, generally either a higher price is bid by the suitor, additional buyers appear, or, in any event, the deal is easily expected to be consummated.

New Listing on Exchange

Once a stock is listed on an exchange or added to an index, the potential for additional interest is enhanced considerably. Index funds are required to include in their portfolios all components in various indexes, and margin requirements are often more attractive once exchange listing is accomplished. For these reasons, the potential audience is often increased significantly. It is not uncommon to witness a price advance even prior to listing, in anticipation of this tendency. Furthermore, many committees of large investment companies restrict investment to only listed stocks—and then only stocks priced in excess of $10. Because of the criteria required for listing approval, these large investors use the listing process and the active requirements to remain listed as additional safeguards to ensure that they are investing prudently. The reverse of this phenomenon occurs when a stock is delisted. Heavy liquidation of delisted stocks, together with the prospects of the company itself failing, are legitimate concerns that are to be respected and expected.

I noticed the same tendency back in the early 1970s, when exchange-listed stock calls were first introduced. It was almost a foregone conclusion that as soon as a call was listed, the underlying security would advance. This pattern was dominant for an extended period of time until the exchange-listed puts were introduced and prices for the underlying stock declined for a short period of time. Unfortunately, this tendency was short-lived. In any case, I remain vigilant to observe the vagaries associated with the introduction of any new product in order to identify any inclination for the pattern to repeat itself.

New Highs–New Lows

Newcomers to a race track can always be expected to bet on the long shots. Typically, those bets have odds over 50-to-1 and almost never win. The smart money— the sophisticated gamblers—conduct their research and bet their money prudently and realistically; any expectations of a long-shot winner are left to inexperienced gamblers. A long shot does occasionally win, amid as many bells and whistles as a big slot machine winner will hear in Las Vegas, but that outcome is the exception. The same concept applies to the stock market. Invariably, inexperienced traders like to focus on yesterday's market winners. History has proven that it is the exception indeed for a strong stock or industry performer in one bull market to repeat its preeminence in a succeeding bull move. Generally, once it has become a fallen angel, it takes a number of market cycles to recover and lead once again. Unsophisticated traders (and some experienced traders) ignore this fact and often become trapped in these losing propositions.

Common sense dictates that, as price declines more and more, owners of a stock incur losses. For the stock to rally significantly to new highs, all the supply created by premature buyers on the way down must be overcome. How many times have you entered a trade only to see price move immediately against you, and then said to yourself that once you break even you will liquidate? Either these buyers must hold their stock positions and not liquidate, or their supply must be absorbed before price can advance. If a stock is making a series of new highs in price, there are no unhappy buyers with losses. Thus, the expectation of liquidation once the trader breaks even is gone. Conceptually, the argument of overhead supply does not exist. My experience of being a stock scavenger was short-lived, once I viewed the prospects in the context of overhead supply. My research proved that stocks making new highs during an overall flat market were candidates for purchase because they were able to defy the laws of gravity displayed by the market indexes. In fact, generally, they were leaders in the market during any period of strength. Conversely, during a sideways market prior to decline, those stocks recording new lows were the leaders on the downside in any market selloff.

Many years ago, I took my research regarding 52-week new highs–new lows and applied a technique that assigned a stock's relative position versus its 52-week high or low. For example, instead of just relying on the list of new highs–new lows as they appeared in the newspaper, I wanted to know precisely how close a given stock, presently at neither a new high nor a new low, was to recording one. Often, the proximity of a stock to recording a new high or a new low is camouflaged. An index I created, the TD New High/Low Index, provided me with a benchmark whereby I could confirm expectations of price breakouts either upside or downside. The index is constructed by dividing the 52-week price movement of a stock by 10, and then ranking the stock on that particular day. If, for example, price records a close today within 10 percent of its 52-week high, then a rating of 10 is assigned to the stock. Conversely, if price records a close less than 90 percent of its 52-week high, then a rating of 1 is assigned to the stock. If the price closes 50 percent less than its 52-week high, then a rating of 5 is assigned to the stock. Next, I calculate a cumulative value and plot this index beneath the price action of a market index to validate price moves and trends and to determine the durability and substance of a trend. This method of evaluating the relative price close versus the price range of the previous year and then calculating a composite index (TD New High/Low Index) to validate overall market moves is a valuable contribution to the library of market indicators. Once again, a basic, widely accepted indicator—new high–new low—is enhanced to create a more complete market indicator. All it took was a little imagination and some creativity.

The other indicators described below are designed to improve on those commonly used by most stock traders. I believe the enhancements I have introduced, as well as the integration of the various approaches into a composite, yield benefits that greatly improve the potential of trading success.

Turbo-Charged Indicators

As is apparent throughout the book, many of the ideas I have presented are improvements on the techniques employed by most traders. My personality is such that I have never been content to accept what everyone else does. I want explanations and logic to substantiate what I do. In most instances, my research confirmed that the widely followed construction and the interpretation of indicators had some validity, but I wanted to exploit them further and make them more effective and valuable with my adaptations. I was comfortable and confident knowing that no one else would be using anything similar unless I shared these indicators with them.

Advance–Decline

Most traders are familiar with advance–decline models. Conventional methods usually run a cumulative index of net advances–declines plotted daily below a particular market index. For over 20 years, I calculated a 5-day average by summing the net advances–declines and then dividing by 5. I also calculated a 13-day average by summing the net advances–declines and then dividing by 13. I established overbought/oversold boundaries for these averages and compared them to a series of other relationships (described below) to arrive at ideal buy or sell opportunities. Generally, I would expect to see the 5-day figure exceed ±450 on the same day that the 13-day figure exceeds ±250.

I perform similar calculations of 5- and 13-day averages for the Dow Jones Industrial Average 30 components. Generally, readings of ±14.0 and ±5.0 for the same-day readings for both the 5-day and the 13-day averages coincide with turning points.

Next, I divide the total advances by the total declines for each day. I sum these values and average them for 5 days and for 13 days. The 5-day figure would have to exceed 1.95, and the 13-day calculation would have to exceed 1.70 on the same day. Conversely, the 5-day figure would have to be below .65 and the 13-day calculation below .95. In turn, these levels would be incorporated into the master model to identify ideal buy and sell entry points.

The next comparison in my overbought/oversold matrix is the ratio of advancing issues/total issues traded. On a 5-day and a 13-day basis, for an ideal oversold reading, I like to see the 5-day below 30 and the 13-day below 35. Conversely, for an ideal overbought reading, I like to see the 5-day above 50 and the 13-day above 45. Integrated into the model constructed by determining ideal overbought/oversold bands for the other indicators, this measure confirms high-risk and low-risk buy and sell zones.

Most people are familiar with the trend index (TRIN) developed by Richard Arms and found on most quotation terminals. This index divides the ratio of advancing to declining issues by the ratio of upside volume to downside volume. I recommend averaging these daily values over 5-day and 13-day periods. If the 5-day value is above 1.35 and the 13-day value is above 1.20, or the 5-day value is below .75 and the 13-day value is below .85 on the same day, and the other relationships in the model confirm, low-risk entry levels can be established.

The last component of the market model is a ratio of the current day's Dow Jones Industrials Close divided by the close of the Dow Jones Industrials Close 55 trading days before. If the ratio is below .89 or above 1.13, usually turning points are identified. Used in conjunction with the other indicators described above, a package of indicators with a respectable track record history is created.

I created this overbought/oversold matrix over 20 years ago. I entered the statistics myself daily. Today, computers simplify this task markedly. I present below a sample of the statistics I accumulate daily.

Date
Total Issues Traded
Advance (Adv)
Decline (Dec)
Net 5-Day 13-Day
Advance
Total
5-Day 13-Day
Advance
Decline
5-Day 13-Day
Net DJIA 5-Day 13-Day
TRIN 5-Day 13-Day
DJIA High Low Close
Momentum Close Today
Close 89 Days Ago
S&P High Low Close
Momentum Close Today
Close 89 Days Ago

Chapter

Options

When I first entered the investment business, the Chicago Board of Options Exchange (CBOE) did not exist. Options were underwritten by brokers and were traded over the counter. Since that time, however, much literature has been written regarding the topic of options. Unfortunately, most information concentrates on procedure and valuation studies. Although some attention is devoted to methods that evaluate market sentiment and that indicate market direction, the extent of this information is woefully incomplete. All the observations I have made originate from personal experiences acquired as a result of numerous forays in the options markets and are not found in textbooks. As I have stated repeatedly throughout this book, "sweating out" personal trades seems to make a trader more alert to potential pitfalls; it also contributes to indelibly fixating on his memory various strategies and opportunities. I will describe my techniques and rules, and, I hope, impart some wisdom that will reduce the likelihood of your trading failure. These techniques have application to both equity and futures options.

Rather than recite numerous incidents and episodes that affected my options trading life, I will share with you the lessons learned. They were acquired as a result of being taught by the "ultimate market teacher"—trading losses. Psychologists have said that many traders possess an unconscious desire to lose in their investments. I am not one of those individuals. I have looked on trading losses, however, as the tuition cost required to be educated in successful market trading. This may sound trite, but I learned from experience. Had someone else offered this information to me years ago, I would have applied it and would have avoided frustration and heavy market losses. Although I was hungry and my appetite for information was voracious, nothing existed to satisfy it.

It has often been said that the only winner in the options game is the writer. Studies have shown that over 80 percent of option traders lose money. When the listed option markets opened, lack of sophistication characterized both the writers and the buyers of the options. The learning curve for the buyers, however, was longer than that for the writers, because little literature was devoted to their plight of trading failure. More than likely, this was a result of the fact that whereas the writers—sellers—were predominantly institutions and floor traders, the buyers were small investors who were naive and did not possess the information and resources the writers did to eliminate these inadequacies.

Emotions and expectations play an important role in options pricing. Strip away these human feelings and the game of options trading becomes much simpler. Many models, developed to ascertain fair values, have been employed by writers for some time and, by using both computers and mechanized strategies, the emotional component has been effectively eliminated and replaced with discipline. My goal was to develop a suitable set of rules for the buyer. Through experience, I accomplished this goal and created a list that is readily accessible anytime I venture into this risky market. Foremost on my mind is the fact that I must control my emotions and must ignore the emotionalism of all my market counterparts who are buying at the same time. My experience suggests that observation of the following rules offers a chance that a trade can turn into a profitable experience. Specifically, I adhere to the following:

1. Only purchase a call option when the overall market is down in price versus the previous day's close;

2. Only purchase a call option when the underlying industry group is down in price versus the previous day's close;

3. Only purchase a call option when the call is down in price versus the previous day's close.

These rules have served me well and, with the exception of replacing the requirement of a down close versus the previous day's close with an up close versus the previous day's close, the rules for purchasing put options have been defined as well. Options trading is difficult enough without allowing your emotions to interfere as well. Together with the simple mathematical comparisons and models presented below, this list should get you on the road to success.

For years, traders have used a simple options ratio to identify sentiment extremes that coincided with price turning points in the underlying securities. Although practitioners have exacted some degree of success in forecasting price reversals, the results are spotty. Simply, what they do is divide overall put volume by overall call volume. My research suggests that approach is deficient for a number of reasons:

1. The assumption is made that for each expiration date and price, there are puts and calls listed;

2. No dollar-weighted adjustment whatsoever is made to the volume statistics;

3. No consideration is given to the interplay of option volume and open interest.

These are critical items that must be addressed to properly assess market sentiment.

Initially, when options were listed on the exchanges, they were limited to calls. Slowly, puts were introduced, but had a trader calculated just the basic put–call ratio, it would certainly have distorted and skewed the results in favor of call volume.

It makes sense that not only is the number of options traded important but so also is the price of these calls and puts. Why should the impact of options priced at one-eighth of a dollar be the same as those priced at five dollars? Consequently, I devised my own ratio of calls to puts by multiplying the volume by the dollar value of each option. I called this ratio the TD Dollar-Weighted Option Ratio. The same band of overbought/oversold that is applied to the conventional approach can be used. However, the results should be more indicative of true sentiment.

Another ingredient in the option equation is often overlooked: the interplay between option volume and open interest. Every time an option is written, open interest expands. By invoking a methodology that incorporates option volume as a percentage of its open interest and in turn dollar-weighting these numbers, another important ratio is created that has predictive value. To get an appreciation for the relationship between volume and open interest, just examine what occurs when the volume in a particular futures market—not options—on a particular day exceeds the open interest on that same day. In essence, what has transpired is that the ownership in that market has been turned over and, consequently, its personality and price characteristics are prone to change. On another level, a similar situation occurs with options.

My personal experience in trading options revealed a situation that is not obvious until one is confronted with its consequences. Specifically, just prior to the market's close on a Friday, I purchased some call options. No news announcements were released prior to the following Monday's reopening. In fact, the underlying security opened much higher. To my dismay, the option's price opened lower than Friday's close and my purchase price. To no avail, I attempted to resolve this perceived dislocation with logic. I consulted with an options expert, and he explained that most option models are updated over the weekend. Typically, the time premium is recalculated at that time. Subsequent to this episode, I concluded that it was prudent to initiate a position on a Monday rather than late on a Friday unless I anticipated that an important event would occur over the weekend and could significantly offset the time premium erosion. This is particularly applicable to options expiring within a month's time.

I have provided you with some of the methods I use to evaluate the sentiment associated with various options markets. Not only can you use these models to evaluate the relative attractiveness of option opportunities, but you can translate this information into opinions regarding the underlying securities. I would hope that you can apply these indicators, as well as the rules for entry, to your advantage by becoming an offensive options trader capable of seizing opportunities as they arise, rather than being defensively disposed struggling to preserve capital.

Chapter

13

"Waldo" Patterns*

In recent years, a fictional cartoon character named Waldo© has been popularized and promoted in books, posters, puzzles, and a game entitled "Where's Waldo?"©. His creator, Martin Handford, has made it a challenge to find Waldo in the midst of hundreds of other cartoon figures. Camouflaged and hidden in the extreme recesses of these pictures is Waldo. His location is difficult to identify, but once shown or discovered it becomes obvious. This exercise reminded me of a similar process I have been involved in for years—identifying, on a chart, price patterns that are obscured and overwhelmed by the price activity surrounding them. Once I became aware of what to look for, however, this process was simple. Consequently, I have labeled these chart relationships and patterns as Waldo patterns. Rather than get into a lengthy discussion regarding their genesis, I will merely highlight their existence and underscore some of the observations I have made regarding their implications. Suffice it to say that I suggest you research these Waldo patterns to determine whether they might play a role in your trading program. Whether you deal in equities, futures, or cash markets, these patterns should convey similar messages.

*Copyright 1987 by Martin Handford, Little, Brown and Company.

When I started in the investment business, I was introduced to all the generally accepted market models, indicators, and techniques. It took approximately one year of hard work and heavy indoctrination by market technicians before I fully grasped the commonly used systems and approaches to market timing. What I learned always appeared good on paper, but to reproduce it and apply it was difficult. My solution was to create original research regardless of the time and expense involved to accomplish it. What surfaced from this research project was the revelation that many of the interpretations assigned to widely followed and often quoted market patterns were just the opposite of what they should have been. This discovery shattered the faith I had in conventional wisdom and forced me to conduct my own research and market timing investigation. I emerged from my self-education with the following principles, which I have adhered to ever since:

1. Most traders believe that increasing volume is an important companion of a genuine price advance. I concur in some instances on a price continuum but my research suggests that such a development is definitely not always the case. For instance, once price has formed a low, I prefer to see light volume because, typically, it suggests a shortage of supply. I defy traders to prove that they correctly purchased the absolute price low. I associate such claims with the many celebrated fish tales. My experience shows that lows are made once the last seller has sold and, by default, price moves sideways to higher. Generally, when heavy upside volume occurs coincident with a new price low, it is of a short covering variety and consequently short-lived. In fact, such a situation generally establishes a price vacuum in which price declines even faster once the decline resumes; this occurs because premature buying has depleted the buying reserve and at the same

time has increased the selling pool. These short covering rallies are typically characterized by their steepness.

Many traders like to relate current upside price action to a reference high recorded some time before. Richard Russell, of Dow Theory Forecasts, made a notable observation many years ago, which I follow to this day. At that time, many traders were focused on a Dow Jones Industrial Average peak recorded many months earlier. The market was advancing on exceptionally heavy volume. Contrary to popular belief, Russell observed that (1) the price movement was running into heavy resistance because of the large volume, and (2) more than likely, price would stall and reverse prior to any penetration of the previous highs. He was correct. I conducted my own research and concluded that an ideal situation arises when price advances and volume is light, suggesting a shortage prior to the price peak. Once the high is exceeded, I look for volume to increase significantly, for two reasons. First, I expect to see short covering and stop loss buying to occur at and above the old price high. Second, trend followers are likely to initiate positions precisely at that price high and above. Consequently, I prefer to see volume explode subsequent to a breakout above a previous high but not before. These same observations apply to price and volume when price declines and the prospects for a previous low's being penetrated are being evaluated.

2. Many traders believe that reversal bottoms and tops are important trading signals. I disagree. I invite you to examine the price charts of most of the actively traded stocks and futures. Generally, price reversals—days in which a low exceeds the previous day's low to the downside and price closes higher, or days

in which price exceeds the previous day's high to the upside and price closes lower—are caused by short-term traders, and prices typically resume their trend once they are completed. Trading days in which price declines and a down close versus the previous day is recorded, or trading days in which price advances and an up close versus the previous day is recorded, are more significant and durable and are likely to occur at price bottoms and tops. There is one pattern that assumes the same significance as the one previously described. In that pattern, a reversal occurs and price closes greater than all previous four closes in the case of an upside reversal or closes less than all previous four closes in the case of a downside reversal.

3. Typically, markets experience a consolidation phase whenever a particular day's price range is more than two times the previous day's price range. This is more apparent if price has been trending for a period of time.

4. Assume the lowest price recorded is 10 or more days ago and, prior to that low, all previous 10 days' lows were higher. Label this low day as the reference day. If the next 2 days are down closes and both record range lows beneath the reference day's close, a price low is likely being formed. To establish a price high, reverse the conditions.

5. Generally, when price closes unchanged versus the previous day's close, price continues to move higher if the previous day's close is up and to move lower if the previous day's close is down.

6. Once a short-term low is formed, by subtracting the difference between that day's close and low and comparing it with the difference

between the previous day's close and low, conclusions regarding the following day's upside potential can be determined. Specifically, if the difference is greater one day ago than two days ago, the prospects are good for a rally, provided that the following day's low does not violate the previous low. Conversely, once a short-term high is formed, by subtracting the difference between the previous day's high and close, conclusions regarding the ensuing day's downside potential can be established. If the difference is greater one day ago than two days ago, the prospects for a decline are good, provided that the following day's high does not violate the previous day's high.

7. A downtrend can be reversed once a price open or close is recorded that exceeds upside the price close four days before the most recent TD Point Low. This must occur within four days of the TD Point Low. If two price gaps are recorded on two days up to and including the first reversal close, the reversal is suspect. Conversely, an uptrend can be reversed once a price open or close is recorded that exceeds downside the price close four days before the most recent TD Point High. This must occur within four days of the TD Point High. If two price gaps are recorded on two days up to and including the first reversal close, the reversal is suspect.

8. If the close 1 day ago is less than the close 5 days ago, and the close today is greater than all previous 7 days' highs but not all previous 11 days' highs, a short-term top is formed. Conversely, if the close 1 day ago is more than the close 5 days ago, and the close today is less than all previous 7 days' lows but not all previous 11 days' lows, a short-term low is formed.

9. Prepare for a potential change in market personality when volume levels on a particular day exceed—or surpass significantly on a percentage basis—historical relationships between volume–open interest levels. This could suggest the potential of an ensuing directional price change.

10. Most trend followers buy when price exceeds upside all previous highs for a prescribed number of days, or sell when price exceeds downside all previous lows for a prescribed number of days. A common practice is to buy once a high exceeds all previous 40 days' highs and to sell once a low exceeds all previous 40 days' lows. Many trend followers remain invested at all times. However, some prefer to take profits and position themselves neutral once price records a 20-day low or a 20-day high. Typically, trend following produces less than 35 percent winners; if portfolio diversification is applied, the likelihood of participating in the trending markets is enhanced considerably.

11. A number of market analysts have observed seasonal price tendencies in the commodities markets. Numerous books have described a number of these observations. What has been often overlooked, however, is the fact that there exists a propensity for stocks to exhibit a similar seasonal behavior. I predict more research will be conducted in this area.

12. Most traders apply the identical overbought/oversold decision rules to bull and bear markets. In an uptrending market, oversold readings occur only for a short time and overbought readings are more dominant. Conversely, in a downtrending market, overbought readings appear for only a short time and oversold readings occur more often. The

overall trend of the market, or the market environment, is a critical factor to consider when interpreting overbought/oversold oscillators. (See Chapter 3.)

13. Prior to the completion of my work regarding trendlines (TD Points and Lines, see Chapter 1), I used a technique to perfect trendline breakout entries. Specifically, I would draw a trendline. If it was an up trendline, I would wait until downside penetration was exhausted. Then I would use the low defined by the sell-off as my sell entry once a subsequent rally was completed. Conversely, I would trace a down trendline and await the completion of the upside penetration. Then I would identify the high defined by the advance as my buy entry once a subsequent decline was completed.

14. Traders like to identify support and resistance levels and often anticipate specific price activity to occur at these price levels. My experience suggests that the concept of support and resistance does have application to stocks, but due to the high turnover in the futures markets, the principle has no application except in intraday trading.

15. One factor overlooked by many traders when operating a market timing system is the significance of specific days of the week, of the month, or of the year. I have conducted some research regarding this area of systems analysis and my findings suggest a more than casual influence.

Conclusion

No trading methodolgy is perfect, and the many methods presented in this book are no exceptions. The techniques I have shared with you have been developed and refined in the most intense and rigorous laboratory conditions imaginable—the trading arena. As I have repeatedly emphasized throughout this book, necessity has truly been the mother of invention in my trading life. Nothing instills the challenge of creativity more than to see personal trading profits erode, only to be replaced with a series of sizable losses.

The goal of successful and profitable trading performance has been an elusive one for me to attain. In those rare instances when my trading juices and adrenalin are flowing most vigorously and my level of confidence is at its peak, I am most vulnerable. One particular example, comes to mind. On a summer day in 1989, many of the mechanical systems I had designed and developed at Tudor generated signals concurrently. Peter Borish, my counterpart at the company, and I were excited about the prospects. What occurred turned out to be one of my most humbling professional experiences. It began as a modestly profitable trade and evolved into a trip into traders' hell—we recorded the largest one-day account drawdown in our trading history. Fortunately, Peter and I had installed money management contingencies that curtailed our losses. Once again, I emphasize the inevitability of encountering just such unexpected events in this business. To reduce their impact, I recommend lessons in money management survival. In addition, I strongly suggest that you prepare a psychological profile highlighting your strengths and weaknesses as a trader, thus enabling you to more easily deal with trading disasters when they arise.

I have attempted to provide you with the tools required to generate profitable trading signals. It is my hope that you will use my research and experience to design and to craft your own trading rules. Nothing would please me more than to read or to hear of a trader's success and accomplishments originating from some ideas presented in this book. I was not afforded this luxury and opportunity when I entered the business many years ago; I had to acquire most of my knowledge from personal trading experiences.

This book is a product and a culmination of those many years of work in a profession in which I am consumed. Larry Bird, the former Boston Celtics' basketball superstar, now retired, remarked subsequent to signing his first post-college multimillion-dollar deal, "It's a good thing Celtics management didn't realize that I love this game so much that I would have played it for nothing." I reiterate precisely the same words regarding my profession. I am confident that should a similar passion for the investment business burn in your life, your trading future is destined to be both emotionally and financially fulfilling and rewarding.

Index